MALTA, GOZO
AND COMINO

a countryside guide
Sixth edition

Douglas Lockhart

SUNFLOWER BOOKS

Sixth edition © 2012
Sunflower Books™
PO Box 36160
London SW7 3WS, UK
www.sunflowerbooks.co.uk

ISBN 978-1-85691-412-3

Mdina Gate

Important note to the reader

We have tried to ensure that the descriptions and maps in this book are
error-free at press date. The book will be updated, where necessary,
whenever future printings permit. It will be very helpful for us to receive
your comments (sent in care of the publishers, please) for the updating
of future printings, and for the Update service described on the inside
back cover of the book.

   We also rely on those who use this book — especially walkers —
to take along a good supply of common sense when they explore.
Conditions change fairly rapidly on the Maltese islands, and ***storm
damage or bulldozing may make a route unsafe at any time***. If the route
is not as we outline it here, and your way ahead is not secure, return to
the point of departure. ***Never attempt to complete a tour or walk under
hazardous conditions!*** Please read carefully the notes on pages 27 to
35, as well as the introductory comments at the beginning of each tour
and walk (regarding road conditions, equipment, grade, distances and
time, etc). Explore ***safely***, while at the same time respecting the beauty
of the countryside.

Cover photograph: farm south of Dingli (Short walk 14-2)
Title page: street name plaque (Vittoriosa, Walk 2)

Photographs: Douglas Lockhart
Touring maps and town plans: Sunflower Books; walking maps adapted
   from maps produced by the Mapping Unit of the Malta Environment
   and Planning Authority, © Mapping Unit, Malta Environment and
   Planning Authority.
A CIP catalogue record for this book is available from the British Library.
Printed and bound in China: WKT Company Ltd

Contents

4   Landscapes of Malta, Gozo and Comino

✿ Preface

Malta, Gozo and Comino attract about 1.3 million tourists each year, most of them from Britain, Italy, Germany and Scandinavia. Many are lured by the typical Mediterranean weather; others see Malta as a change from the Spanish 'Costas', while British ex-servicemen and their families, once stationed here, come back for a nostalgic look at how things have changed. Not everyone stays around the hotel pools or heads for the nearest beach and, during my visits, I have been pleasantly surprised to meet so many people like myself touring or walking in the countryside. The Maltese landscape offers rich rewards for those who enjoy exploring: interests in ancient and modern history, military and ecclesiastical architecture, geology, and flora are all well catered for. If this is your first visit to Malta, sampling a few of these walks will whet your appetite for many more return visits!

Landscapes of Malta, Gozo and Comino is divided into three main sections, each with its own introduction. **Motorists** will visit picturesque fishing villages, ancient ruins, high sea-cliffs, churches, and peaceful byways. **Picnickers** will be able to sample more than 30 lovely picnic spots, each of them surrounded by spectacular scenery or interesting man-made features. **Walkers** can enjoy gentle ambles or more strenuous hikes occupying a whole day; the walks visit the most exhilarating and spectacular landscapes on the three islands.

The history of the Maltese Islands dates back to Neolithic times, when settlers came from nearby Sicily, bringing with them domestic animals, agriculture and pottery. Since then the Phoenicians, Carthaginians, Romans, Arabs, Knights of St John, the French (for just two years), and the British have all left their marks of ownership. The islands are rich in prehistoric remains, among them the vast megalithic sanctuaries at Hagar Qim on Malta and Ggantija on Gozo, and tombs like the Hypogeum at Paola (Malta). More recent rulers, such as the Knights of St John, were responsible for building the impressive city of Valletta, and the defensive walls that guarded the city and its Grand Harbour against invaders are architectural masterpieces. The countryside is peppered with watchtowers and forts: some were built in

5

Victorian times; others, dating from World War II, reflect Malta's strategic position in the Mediterranean. The Maltese are a deeply religious people, and imposing churches and delightful chapels, many of which are open to the public, can be found everywhere. Valletta's National Museum of Archaeology, Palace of the Grand Masters of the Order of St John, and War Museum are well worth visiting.

Malta has been independent since 1964, becoming a republic ten years later. The last British forces left in 1979. Malta joined the European Union in 2004. The Republic consists of three main islands, Malta, Gozo and Comino, as well as a number of small uninhabited islets. Malta's land area is only 246 sq km (95 sq mi) and that of Gozo 67 sq km (26 sq mi), yet the Maltese Islands are home to a population of 413,000 — making them one of the most densely-populated areas in the world. Fortunately for lovers of the countryside, most Maltese live near Valletta and in a dozen other small towns, leaving much open countryside and unspoilt coast.

Over the centuries the Maltese people have come into contact with many nations and cultures that have tried to dominate them. As a result they are one of the most cosmopolitan of peoples. Paradoxically, the Maltese language has survived, although English is the co-official language and is spoken by almost 90% of the population.

Acknowledgements

Many thanks to Leslie Vella, Suzanne Cassar Dimech and Janet Grech of the Malta Tourism Authority for help with this Sixth edition. Thanks also to Sue Ashton for her contribution to the first two editions, and to the many 'Landscapers' who have made helpful comments.

Useful books

Frans A Attard, *The Maze: Comprehensive guide to streets of Malta & Gozo*, Uptrend Publishing, Birkirkara, 7th edition, 2010

Brian Blouet, *The Story of Malta*, Valletta, Progress Press, 6th edition, 1997

Leonard Mahoney, *5000 Years of Architecture in Malta*, Valletta Publishing, Valletta, 1996

Athanassios Migos (ed), *The Fortifications of Malta [by Quentin Hughes]*, Nearchos Publications, Rock Ferry, Wirral, 1997

Paul Murphy (ed), *Malta — Insight Guide*, Singapore, APA Publications, updated 4th edition, 2007

Geoffrey A Ross and Jonathan Beacon, *The Maltese Islands from the Air*, Proud Publishing, Balzan, 1994

Ray C Zammit (ed), *The Victoria Lines: Souvenir Guide*, Progress Press, Valletta, 1996

Getting about

A **hired car** is undoubtedly the most useful way of exploring Malta and Gozo. International companies are represented in the main tourist centres and offer a range of modern cars. Local garages also have cars for hire, but these tend to be older. Rental prices are low and generally less expensive than UK rates.

Coach tours operate from hotels throughout the year and will take you to the major attractions on Malta and Gozo; they offer a useful introduction to history and scenery, but you won't get off the beaten track.

Public bus services are run by Arriva Bus Malta Ltd. A fleet of modern buses serve most areas of Malta and Gozo on a regular basis. Prices are relatively low, and if you intend walking on most days of your stay, I recommend purchasing a 7-day ticket. Most of the walks in this book can be reached by bus, and there are frequent connections from the resorts to the bus terminus near City Gate in Valletta. Bus services in Gozo have a basic hourly frequency, while the most direct service between the harbour at Mgarr and the main town of Victoria (Route 301) operates every half hour. I urge you to study Arriva's very detailed website (www.arriva.com.mt) carefully — either before arriving in Malta or at your hotel. The site incorporates a 'journey planner' facility in which alternative routings and corresponding journey times are shown and timetables for all routes. It also has an update section detailing any service changes. Most walks make use of the mainline, direct and Gozo route categories. In addition there are express services from the airport and Valletta to some destinations, park and ride services from

Comino ferry

hubs at Pembroke near St Julian's, Marsa and Floriana, and late services at the weekend from St Julian's for those who might wish to combine night-life and walking.

Taxis operate from the major centres in Malta and, on Gozo, they are readily hired at Mgarr Harbour. Rates are controlled by the authorities and most taxi garages advertise fixed fares to popular destinations. Taxis are a comfortable and economical way of exploring routes not taken by coach tours, especially if the cost is shared.

Motorcycles and **bicycles** are an inexpensive way of getting around Gozo and can be hired in Victoria.

Inter-island ferries: The Malta–Gozo service is operated by roll-on/roll-off vehicle ferries belonging to the Gozo Channel Company, Channel House, Mgarr, Gozo (www.gozochannel.com). The Comino Hotel operates a scheduled boat service from Cirkewwa and Mgarr to the hotel pier when the hotel is open (generally late March to early November; www.cominohotel.com). Weather permitting, a service between Marfa (opposite the Riviera Hotel), Cirkewwa (near the Gozo ferry terminal) and the Blue Lagoon in Comino is operated throughout the year by United Comino Ferries (www.cominoferries.com). For telephone numbers and journey times on all these services, see page 133.

Sea plane service between Malta and Gozo: A sea plane service operates several times a day between Valletta Waterfront (Sea Passenger Terminal) and Mgarr Harbour (www.harbourairmalta.com).

Printed timetables are available for ferry crossings to Gozo and Comino (United Comino Ferries). On pages 131-133 you will find bus timetables and ferry information covering the services used for the walks and picnics in this book, as well as services connecting the resorts with Valletta. Note that on **Malta** there are differences in service frequencies depending on day of the week and, in some cases, the season; space restrictions do not allow us to print all timetable variations. The heading 'Last bus' applies to Monday to Friday services. **Gozo** buses keep to the same timetable every day of the year. Please do not rely *solely* on the timetables in this book; check details of ferry sailings (especially if visiting Comino) and obtain the latest bus information from Arriva's website or staff at one of the termini. A missed connection could spoil your day.

Bus departure points are shown on the town plans for Valletta (page 38), Rabat (page 44) and Victoria on Gozo (with the Gozo touring map inside the back cover).

☀ Picnicking

Picnicking on the Maltese Islands is very much an informal activity, as there are only a few locations, such as belvederes, with benches. However, the islands abound in spectacular settings on cliff-tops or delightful little coves where a private picnic can be enjoyed.

The following five pages contain all the information you need to get to more than 30 lovely picnic places. *Picnic numbers correspond to walk numbers,* so that you can quickly find the general location on the islands by looking at the touring maps (on which the area of each walk is outlined in white).

Many of these picnic spots are very easily accessible by bus, car or taxi and require only a short walk. Some, however, are best suited to those of you out for a ramble (for instance Picnics 7b, 21b, and 26d). I include walking times, transport details (🚌: how to get there by bus; 🚗: where to park), a map reference, and information about the views or setting. The location of the picnic spot is shown on the corresponding *walking map* by the symbol *P*. Several of the picnic places are illustrated.

Please remember that when one of the picnic suggestions is off the beaten track, you will want to wear sensible shoes and take a sunhat (○ indicates a picnic in

Blue Lagoon, Comino (Picnic 27)

full sun). It's a good idea to take along a plastic sheet as well, in case the ground is damp or prickly.

If you are travelling to your picnic by public transport, use the Arriva journey planner (see page 7) to verify the timetables on pages 131-133. You may be able to obtain similar information from Arriva staff if your journey begins at one of the major centres (Valletta, Sliema Ferries or Bugibba on Malta; Victoria on Gozo). If your outward and return journeys use the same service, your driver may know the timetable for later in the day. *Always* check return ferry times on your outward trip, particularly from Comino and from Gozo if you need a bus connection at Cirkewwa.

If you are travelling by car, be extra vigilant off the main roads: farmers and their animals, and children in village streets may be unaware of traffic. Park well off the road, without damaging plants or blocking a road or track.

All picnickers should remember to read the Country code on page 34 and go quietly in the countryside.

4a Malta: Mellieha Bay (map pages 46-47) ○

by car or bus: up to 5min on foot
🚌 Park on the esplanade at Mellieha Bay; 🚐 11, 41 to Ghadira Police Station
One of Malta's best beaches. No shade, but there are several bars and restaurants nearby.

4b Malta: Marfa Ridge (map pages 46-47) 🛱

by car: up to 5min on foot; by bus: 40min on foot
🚌 Park at one of the picnic sites along the ridge road; 🚐 11, 41: alight at the crossroads near the Red Tower and follow the ridge road eastwards (see Short walk 4-2 on page 47).
One of the Malta's few organised picnic sites (signposted). Tables under the trees; shade. Views to St Paul's Islands.

4c Malta: Armier Bay (map pages 46-47, photo page 48) ○

by car: up to 5min on foot; by bus: 5-40min on foot
🚌 Park at Armier Bay (the third

turn left off the Marfa Ridge road); 🚐 11, 41 to the road junction near the Red Tower (with a 40min walk to the beach; see Short walk 4-2, page 47).
Plenty of parking at this pleasant sandy beach, and a few bars and restaurants. A popular spot with the Maltese on Sundays and in the summer holidays.

5 Malta: Red Tower (map pages 46-47) ○

by car : up to 5min on foot by bus: 5-10min on foot
🚌 Park off the side of the road near the tower, on Marfa Ridge; 🚐 11, 41: as Picnic 4c, then follow Walk 5 on page 50.
Fine views of Mellieha to the south and Gozo to the north. Note: it can be very windy here!

6 Malta: GOLDEN BAY (map page 54) ○

by car: 5-10min on foot by bus: 5-10min on foot
🚌 Park near the Golden Sands Hotel; 🚐 23 or 102 to Ghajn

Tuffieha terminus; use the map on page 54 to get to the beach. *Good sandy beach. No shade.*

7a Malta: Triq Selmun (map pages 58-59) ○

by car: no walking
by bus: 10min on foot
🚗 Park at Selmun hamlet;
🚌 11, 41, X6: alight at the Mellieha (Belle View) interchange (near the roundabout on the outskirts of Mellieha), then follow the access road towards Selmun hamlet and the hotel. *A belvedere with seats and a fine view to St Paul's Bay.*

7b Malta: Mgiebah Bay (map pages 58-59, photo page 12) ○

by car: 20-25min on foot
by bus: 40min on foot
🚗 Park near Selmun Palace;
🚌 11, 41, X6: as Picnic 7a above. Follow the start of Walk 7 (page 56) to reach the beach. *This is a peaceful little cove flanked by rocky headlands.*

7c Malta: Mistra Bay (map pages 58-59) ○

by car: up to 5min on foot
by bus: 15-20min on foot
🚗 Park at Mistra Bay; 🚌 11, 41: alight at Mistra Village Apartments; use the map on pages 58-59) to reach the beach. *A sheltered bay: good sunbathing, swimming and picnicking.*

10a Malta: Victoria Lines (map pages 64-65, photo page 69) ○

by car: up to 5min on foot
by bus: 15min on foot
🚗 Park at the Lines: Take the Gharghur road (1km south of Bahar ic-Caghaq). Drive past the chapel shown on pages 66-67 and Villa Suzie (both on your left), then turn right on a narrow road to the Lines; 🚌 21, 23: alight in Gharghur village.

Follow the road towards Madliena, then turn left on a road just 30m/yds before Villa Suzie. *Magnificent views; popular at weekends with the local people.*

10b Malta: Victoria Lines Garden (map pages 64-65) ○

by car: up to 15min on foot
by bus: 25min on foot
🚗 and 🚌 as Picnic 10a. Follow notes for Picnic 10a, but continue 10 minutes more, to reach another small garden with seats. *Good views of the north coast.*

11a Malta: Bingemma Gap (map pages 74-75, photo page 69) ○

by car: up to 5min on foot
by bus: 40-50min on foot
🚗 Park by the chapel at Bingemma Gap, northwest of Rabat; 🚌 51, 52 or 53 to Rabat (Saqqajja), then either take a taxi to Bingemma Gap, or walk there via the Busugrilla roundabout (see map). Or 🚌 23 to Mgarr and 🚌 102 to Bingemma hamlet, then 15 minutes on foot. *Picnic by the chapel; wonderful views over all of northern Malta.*

11b Malta: Lippija Tower (map pages 70-71) ○

by car: 10-15min on foot
by bus: 25min on foot
🚗 Park off the side of the track to the tower (the track runs northwest from the Gnejna Bay road); 🚌 23: alight in Mgarr and follow Short walk 11-2 (page 69). *Magnificent seascapes, but keep away from the edge of the cliff!*

12a Malta: Mtarfa, Belvedere on Triq Sir Philip Pullicino (map page 83)

by car: no walking
by bus: 3min on foot
🚗 Park at the belvedere; 🚌 51: alight at the junction of Triq

L-Imtarfa and Triq il-Konti F T
Castelletto and follow the latter
until turning left at its junction
with Triq Sir Philip Pullicino.
*Seats partly shaded by canopy,
fine views of the Qlejgha Valley.*

12b Malta: Gnejna Bay (map pages 74-75) ○

*by car: up to 5min on foot
by bus: 40min on foot*
🚗 Park at Gnejna Bay; 🚌 23,
102: alight in Mgarr village and
follow the road to the bay.
*A pleasant bay, guarded by
spectacular cliffs.*

13 Malta: Public Garden at Targa Gap (map pages 78-79)

by car or bus: up to 5min on foot
🚗 Park on the track from the
Victoria Lines; 🚌 31, 41: alight
at Targa Gap.
*Public gardens on the outskirts
of Mosta with good views of the
countryside and St Paul's Bay.*

15 Malta: Rabat (Tal-Virtu) (map pages 88-89) ○

*by car or taxi: no walking
by bus: 5min on foot.*
🚗 Park at the viewpoint: on
entering Rabat (from Valletta/
Zebbug), drive along Triq Nikol

Saura and Triq Gorg Borg
Olivier, turn left on Triq Tal-
Virtu, and park 400m along, on
the left; 🚌 52, 53: alight at the
junction of Triq Tal-Virtu and
Triq Gorg Borg Olivier (the third
bus stop in Rabat after the bus
has climbed the steep hill into
town). Follow the blue signpost
'Seminarju' at this junction, to
reach the viewpoint.
*Seats at this viewpoint, opposite
the Apostolic Nunciature, with
wonderful views of the
surrounding countryside to
Mosta and as far as Valletta.*

16 Malta: Buskett Gardens (map pages 88-89, photo page 92)

*by car: up to 5min on foot
by bus: 5-10min on foot*
🚗 Park at the Buskett Gardens;
🚌 107 to Buskett
*Picnic anywhere in the unusual
gardens. Shade of pines, citrus
and a host of other trees. A
popular spot at weekends.*

17a Malta: Ghar Lapsi (map pages 94-95)

*by car: up to 5min on foot
by bus: 1min on foot*
🚗 Park at Ghar Lapsi; 🚌 109 to
Ghar Lapsi
*A very sheltered spot in windy
weather; interesting fishermen's
boats and jetties. Some shade at
the huddle of boat-houses.*

17b Malta: Wied Iz-Zurrieq (map pages 94-95)

*by car: up to 5min on foot
by bus: 5min on foot*
🚗 Park in the car park at the
entrance to this fishing village;
🚌 201: alight at the main road.
It's a stiff climb back up!
*A spectacular steep-sided valley
provides the backdrop, and the*

Mgiebah Valley (Picnic 7a)

Salt pans at Blata l-Bajda (Walk 7)

fishing boats ferrying passengers
to the Blue Grotto are a constant
source of interest. Some shade
at nearby village bars.

21a Malta: Gardens, St Thomas Bay (map page 105) ○

by car: 2min on foot
by bus: no walking
🚗 Park close to the gardens;
🚌 91: alight at the bus stop just
before the San Tomaso bar on
Triq Il-Qalet.
*Pleasant terraced gardens over-
looking the bay. Nearby bars
and restaurants (some seasonal).
Small sandy beach. Very popular at weekends.*

21b Malta: Il-Qala-t-Tawwalija (map page 105) ○

only by car: 5-10min on foot
🚗 Park at the Ta' Kalanca car
park at Delimara Point: this
bar/restaurant is closed; *leave
nothing of value in your car.*
Then see the map on page 105.
A small sheltered cove.

22 Malta: Blata l-Bajda (map page 109) ○

by car: 1min on foot
by bus: 5min on foot
🚗 Park on the seafront (Dawret
ix-Xatt); 🚌 3: alight at the
terminus in Xghajra.
*Salt pans, swimming possible,
and a small bar which is
popular with the local people.*

23a Gozo: Belvedere on Triq Saghtrija, Zebbug (map pages 112-113) ○

by car: no walking
by bus: 10min on foot
🚗 Park just off Triq Saghtrija;
🚌 309: alight at Zebbug church
*Superb views of Gozo's remote
northwest coast from a hilltop
viewpoint on the edge of the
village. Seats. No shade.*

23b Gozo: Xwieni Bay (map pages 112-113, photo page 113) ○

by car: up to 5min on foot
by bus: 5-10min on foot
🚗 Park at Xwieni Bay.
🚌 306 to Qbajjar, then on foot
*Picturesque cove with salt pans
and dramatic cliffs.*

24a Gozo: Xlendi (map pages 116-117)

by car: up to 5min on foot
by bus: 5min on foot
🚗 Park in Xlendi village; 🚌
306 from Victoria to Xlendi
*There are any number of
water's-edge picnic spots on the
way to Xlendi Tower. Some
shade near the harbour bars and
restaurants.*

24b Gozo: Dwejra Bay (map pages 116-117, photos pages 26 and 115) ○

by car: 5-10min on foot
by bus: 2min on foot
🚗 Park at Dwejra and refer to
the notes on page 118.
🚌 302 to Dwejra
*Wear sturdy shoes to explore
the rock formations and Inland
Sea. Wonderful coastal scenery,
but little shade except at the
Inland Sea.*

Cliffs overlooking Dahlet Qorrot

25 Gozo: Mgarr ix-Xini (map pages 120-121) ○

only by car: 2min on foot
🚗 Limited parking on the minor road from Sannat and Xewkija, on the southwest side of the valley.
Fjord-like inlet; very sheltered; fishermen's boat houses.

26a Gozo: Hondoq ir-Rummien (map pages 124-125) ○

only by car: up to 5min on foot
🚗 Park at Hondoq ir-Rummien, southeast of Qala.
A water pipeline and a disused quarry nearby don't detract from this secluded little bay overlooking Comino.

26b Gozo: Dahlet Qorrot (map pages 124-125) ○

only by car: up to 5min on foot
🚗 Park at Dahlet Qorrot, northeast of Nadur.
There's pleasant picnicking near the boat houses, but no shade.

26c Gozo: Triq San Blas, Nadur (map pages 124-125)

by car or taxi: no walking
by bus: 15-20min on foot
🚗 Park nearby; do not attempt to drive down the narrow road

14

to San Blas Bay; 🚌 303, 322: alight at Nadur church.
A garden with seats, some shaded by a canopy, on the outskirts of the village, overlooking the San Blas Valley.

26d Gozo: San Blas Bay (map pages 124-125)

only by car: 15-20min on foot
🚗 Park on the northern outskirts of Nadur village; don't try to drive down the steep narrow road, as turning is very difficult.
Delightfully secluded; ideal for swimming. Shade by the boat houses.

26e Gozo: Ir-Ramla (map pages 124-125, photo page 33) ○

by car: up to 5min on foot
by bus: 2min on foot
🚗 Park at Ir-Ramla; 🚌 302 to Ir-Ramla
Good sand and historic sites nearby. Little shade; not recommended in windy weather.

27 Comino: Blue Lagoon (map page 129, photo page 9) ○

by boat: up to 5min on foot
⛴ See page 128 for details.
Picnic on the rocks. There's very good swimming, but no shade.

☀ Touring

Car hire in the Maltese Islands is inexpensive and an invaluable way of getting to the more isolated areas. Those staying in the north and the southeast of Malta will find a car especially useful, as it will save considerable time over the public bus. Although **driving is on the left-hand side of the road**, it can be a tiring experience, especially in the hot sun. Parking in town centres in Malta can be very difficult.

The main roads are very heavily trafficked. These have received considerable investment in recent years, and pavements and cycle lanes have been added when roads have been rebuilt. However, in towns hazards such as double parking, construction vehicles and equipment parked at the roadside, speed cameras, potholes, and complicated junctions abound, so keep alert at all times.

Secondary roads are an extremely mixed bag: some are perfectly motorable, but many wind between stone walls and afford only restricted views. These roads tend to be poorly surfaced and suffer from limited maintenance. I would *not* advise extensive use of secondary roads. The touring map shows all the roads I would recommend for motoring, but you may find it interesting to refer to the large-scale *walking maps* while touring, because of their wealth of detail.

The touring notes are brief: they include little history or information available in standard guides or tourist office literature. I concentrate instead on 'logistics': distances, road conditions, the finest viewpoints, and clear directions as to the best route (where signposts might let you down). Above all, the touring notes emphasise possibilities for **walking** and **picnicking**. The symbol *P* alerts you to a picnic spot; see pages 9-14. While some of the suggestions for walks and picnics may not be suitable during a car tour, you may find a landscape that you would like to explore at leisure another day.

The fold-out touring map is designed to be held out opposite the touring notes and contains all the information you will need outside the towns. **Town plans** are included for Valletta (page 38), the Three Cities (page 40), Rabat/Mdina (page 44) and Victoria on Gozo (with the Gozo touring map inside the back cover).

Both of the tours on Malta start and finish in the main resort area of Sliema; the Gozo tour begins at Mgarr harbour. However any of the tours can be joined from other points without difficulty.

Symbols used in the touring notes correspond to those on the touring map; see map key for explanation.

Some points worth noting

- Before setting off, check that the car has a jack and spare tyre (**punctures** are a common occurrence).
- **Speed limits** are as follows: 35 kmph in built-up areas, but occasionally 25 or 30 kmph; 50, 60 or 70 kmph elsewhere.
- Priority on **roundabouts** is given to traffic already negotiating the roundabout.
- In the event of an **accident**, removal of the car (even if it is blocking the traffic) before the arrival of the police will invalidate the insurance.
- **Allow plenty of time** for visits; the times given only allow for very brief stops at viewpoints.
- **Telephones** are found in most villages. Public **WC**s are more widely available than in most European countries; others are found in bars.
- In towns only **park** your car where permitted.
- **Petrol stations** are open between 06.00 and 18.00. Automatic machines provide 'out of hours' service at many stations. A programme of upgrading petrol stations is currently in progress.
- **All motorists should read the Country code on page 34 and go quietly in the countryside.**

Harbour at St Julian's (Car tour 1)

Car tour 1 MALTA: RESORTS, BEACHES, AND HISTORIC TOWNS

Sliema • Salina Bay • Mellieha • Cirkewwa • Golden Bay • Mgarr • Bingemma Gap • Rabat • Mdina • Mosta • Naxxar • San Gwann • Sliema

71km/44mi; about 2h30min driving

On route: Picnics (**P** symbol; see pages 9-14): 4a, (4b, 4c, 5), 6, (7a), 7b, 7c, (10a, 10b), 11a, (11b), 12a, 12b, (13), 15; Walks 3-15

A leisurely tour on asphalted roads of variable quality, with some superb views and coastal scenery. The western ridge and coast roads tend to be narrow and steep, requiring especially careful driving.

This drive visits the northern and western parts of the island and includes two contrasting coastlines — one low and rocky, attracting much tourism development, and the other bounded by high perpendicular cliffs with few access points to the sea. The second half of the tour passes through the interior, where the rural landscape features a succession of ridges and valleys before arriving at the historic walled town of Mdina. From there it is only a short journey back to the waterfront at Sliema.

Head northwest out of Sliema on the coast road to **St Julian's★** (2.7km 🏨✕🏪), a fast-developing resort area boasting many five-star hotels. Just up from the bay, fork left (following signposting for St Andrew's) and then turn right on the main road at the top of the rise (signposted to St Andrew's, St Paul's Bay, Mellieha). You are now on the wide coastal road and heading for quieter countryside, *but take care:* this is reputed to be one of Malta's most dangerous roads.

Just past the old Pembroke Barracks, a road on your left leads up to Gharghur (**P**10a, 10b). Continue straight on to **Bahar ic-Caghaq**. Walk 10 ends here, having descended from the Victoria Lines. Continue on around to **Ghallis Point** and Tower (10.5km 🏛), setting for Walk 9. Fishing from the rocks, as well as the marine park, provide attractions in this coastal area which slopes gently to the sea. **Salina Bay**, with its salt pans, is the next port of call.

The rash of modern development at Bugibba appears on the skyline. (It is possible to divert into Bugibba, Malta's response to the Spanish 'Costas', by turning off right and then bearing right again to Qawra Point. From there continue on through Bugibba, rejoining the road at St Paul's Bay.)

Ignore the bypass and go through the town of **St Paul's Bay** (San Pawl il-Bahar; 14.5km ⛰✕🚍), to enjoy the local colour. The small harbour is worth a visit — it's a piece of old Malta, tucked away from the new development. Carry on through **Xemxija**, where Walks 7 and 8 end. A small road on the left (signposted Mistra) takes us under the main road and down to **Mistra Bay** (18.5km 📷**P**7b). The road winds through a gentle agricultural landscape to a secluded bay.

Return to the main road, which winds its way through several hairpin bends up to the village of **Mellieha** (22km ✝✕🚍📷 and access to **P**7a). There are several new hotels and restaurants in the main street and many characterful local shops. Just past the large reddish-coloured church, there is a fine viewpoint. The road descends to **Ghadira** and **Mellieha Bay★** (23.5km ⛰✕ **P**4a), a very popular sandy beach. Walk 6 starts here, and

The beautiful old Casa del Tesoriere in pristine Mdina's Pjazza Tas-Sur

Walk 5 ends here. The Ghadira Nature Reserve is off to the left.

Drive up to the next ridge now, via more hairpin bends. From here diversions (not included in the mileage) may be made to the left (to the Red Tower; ***P***5) or to the right, to Armier Bay (***P***4c; photograph page 48) or the Madonna statue at the end of Marfa Ridge (⛩***P***4b). To reach Armier Bay take the third turning left off the ridge road, near a shrine.

The main road continues to the Gozo ferry harbour at **Cirkewwa** (32km ▲▲), but you can visit Paradise Bay by branching off left just before the hotel of the same name.

Retrace your route from Cirkewwa to the roundabout at Ghadira (36km, just below the Mellieha Ridge. For a different perspective, take the bypass this time and, towards the top of the ridge, at the roundabout on the outskirts of Mellieha village, turn right (signposted Ghajn Tuffieha). This narrow road winds through ridge and valley country (past the track to the Ghajn Snuber Tower) to the agricultural village of **Manikata** (40km). Then it descends to the crescent-shaped sandy beach of **Golden Bay★** (▲▲✕ ***P***6b), where Walks 6 and 11 end.

From Golden Bay turn right towards the next bay (Ghajn Tuffieha), left at a T-junction, and then right again onto the Ta' Saliba/Zebbieh road. At Ta' Saliba turn right for **Mgarr** (45km ✝⛽) and its distinctive domed church, shown on page 20. In the village centre, turn right and descend to **Gnejna Bay** (47.5km ***P***12), where you'll see colourful boat houses and dramatic rock formations. Walk 12 nears its end here.

From the bay return to Mgarr. Under 2km uphill you pass the turn-off left to the Lippija Tower (***P***11b), one of the settings for Walk 11. Drive straight through Mgarr and take a road on the right on the outskirts of the village. This steep narrow road takes you through the imposing Dwejra Lines at **Bingemma Gap** (53km 📷), the starting point for Walk 11 and about halfway along the route of Walk 13. The views from the little chapel (***P***11a) are wonderful and well worth a stop (photograph page 69). Descend from the ridge, crossing over the head of the Chadwick Lakes (Walk 13) and making for Rabat.

Arriving at the **Busugrilla roundabout*** opposite the Nigred housing estate (starting point for Walks 12 and 14), continue to historic **Mdina★** (57km ✝M▲▲✕📷). Parking is available near the Roman Villa. The 'silent city' of Mdina, into which traffic is restricted, is one of Malta's most beautiful places. Walk 3 ambles round Mdina and its suburb, **Rabat** (✝✕⛽), where there are catacombs and more imposing buildings. Walk 15 begins at Tal-Virtu, in the southeastern corner of Rabat (***P***15).

Leaving Mdina, descend the hill

*I highly recommend a detour from the Busugrilla roundabout to the remote western coast: follow the signs for Fiddien Bridge. The road runs parallel with the *wied* initially and eventually descends to the foot of high vertical cliffs via a series of hairpin bends. The spectacular scenery is exhilarating. Allow 13km return (not included in the mileage) and beware: some maps do not show this road system correctly.

Mosta Dome and (left) inside the church, decorated for Christmas

and follow the signs to **Mosta★** (61km ♨✕🚻⊕), the starting point for Walk 13. Mosta's enormous domed church (said to be the fourth largest unsupported rotunda in the world) is your next target. Short walk 8 and Walk 13 end at Targa Gap on the outskirts of town, where there are public gardens offering fine views of St Paul's Bay (*P*13). From Mosta Dome fight your way through the traffic,

following the road signs for St Paul's Bay, to a roundabout on the outskirts of the town. Follow signposts to Naxxar at both this roundabout and the next one. Turn right into **Naxxar** at 64.5km, passing the residence of the British High Commissioner. Under 2km along, turn left at a roundabout (signposted to San Gwann/Sliema). Driving through this conurbation is always difficult. On the outskirts of **San Gwann** (67.5km), which is a Maltese 'new town', turn right for Gzira/Msida, ignoring the road straight ahead, signposted for Sliema. (The road straight ahead *would* get you back, but it is a more complicated route.) Continue to follow the Msida/Gzira signs into the fashionable area of Kappara, until you reach a roundabout on the Sliema regional road. If you carry straight on here, you will come to the Gzira seafront and then turn left for Sliema (71km).

Car tour 2 MALTA: ANTIQUITIES, FISHING VILLAGES AND GARDENS

Sliema • Hypogeum • Marsascala • Marsaxlokk • Wied iz-Zurrieq
• Hagar Qim • Ghar Lapsi • Buskett Gardens • San Anton Gardens
• Sliema

74km/46mi; about 2h30min
driving
On route: Picnics (**P** symbol; see
pages 9-14): 16, 17a, 17b;
Walks 14, 16-22. (Picnics 21a,

21b and 22 are not far off the
touring route.)
*A comprehensive tour on roads
of reasonable quality, with
varied and interesting scenery.*

This drive complements Tour 1 and shows you the rest of Malta. Pretty fishing villages, fascinating ancient monuments, historic gardens, and the Blue Grotto combine to make this a really memorable drive.

From Sliema hug the interesting little creeks southwards to **Pietà** (4km), where one of the Gozo cargo ferries may be lying at anchor. Continue by looping underneath the Floriana/Marsa road, then head uphill to join it. Follow signs for Marsa and, on approaching an industrial estate, signs for Paola (⊕). You skirt the shipyard near high-density housing estates.
The **Hypogeum** (8km **fi**) is signposted: the vast underground tombs and temple are well worth a visit. The nearby Neolithic temples at Tarxien (less than a kilometre from the Hypogeum) are also highly recommended. Your ongoing route follows signposting for Fgura and Zabbar; a mosque provides a landmark, indicating that you are on the correct road. Pass the Hompesch Arch (11.5km) and, on the outskirts of Zabbar, turn right for the picturesque fishing village of Marsascala (signposted).
Marsascala★ (15km **fi 🔺 ✕ 🖃**) is an ideal spot to recuperate from all the heavy traffic and indulge in a fish lunch at one of the many waterfront cafés. Walk 21 starts out here; Walk 22 begins and ends here. Take heart, the roads are relatively quiet from now on. Turn left along the

promenade towards the former Jerma Palace Hotel and St Thomas Tower. After passing the hotel, turn right, then left, on the road leading down to St Thomas Bay, where there are more restaurants (✕**P**21a).
Turn right to **Zejtun** (19.5km **fi**), a typical and unspoilt large Maltese village with an impressive late 17th-century church, worth seeing for its richly-painted interior. The route through this village is also complicated: after passing the bus terminus on the eastern outskirts, bear right at the first church, skirt around the main church in the centre, and then follow signs for Tarxien — to escape Zejtun from the west. Eventually you should come to the main Valletta/Birzebbuga road. Turn left here towards Birzebbuga, then turn left again, driving through vineyards to **Marsaxlokk★** (24km **fi ✕ 🖃**), the attractive village shown on pages 102-103. Walk 20 begins here, and Walk 21 ends here.
Take the coastal road out of Marsaxlokk to St George's Bay, passing the Ferretti Battery. On reaching the main road, turn right for the archaeological site and museum of **Ghar Dalam** (**fi**; under 1km return) or go

straight across to the fortified Bronze Age village of **Borg in-Nadur★** (27.5km 🏛). The latter is visited on Walk 20.

Keep to the coastal road via **Birzebugga** into **Pretty Bay**, which unfortunately has now acquired an industrial backdrop. Head towards Kalafrana but, at 30km, follow the main road around to the right, towards the old Hal Far airfield (now an industrial estate). Just beyond the airfield turn left for Zurrieq, a small town which poses yet more navigational problems: at about 36km, on the outskirts,

turn left (opposite St Agata Church) into the centre of **Zurrieq**. The main church is reached in under a kilometre (37km ✝🚌). Continue straight on (circling the church) to the bypass. Turn left on reaching the bypass and follow signs for Wied iz-Zurrieq/Blue Grotto. The road provides some spectacular views on the descent to **Wied iz-Zurrieq★** (40km ✗📷 *P*17b), and the little inlet is an exciting picnicking spot. Walk 17 ends here.

Retrace your route uphill and, in about a kilometre, turn left for

The silver domes of Dingli church (left) and view northeast along the Dingli Cliffs (above)

the prehistoric temples of **Hagar Qim** and **Mnajdra** (🏛) — famous for their lovely setting close to the sea, from where they look out to the off-shore island of Filfa (a nature reserve). The road continues west to a roundabout; turn left here to the picturesque hamlet sheltering in a bay under the cliffs, **Ghar Lapsi** (46.5km ✕🖼*P*17a) — a delightful picnicking and swimming spot visited on Walk 17.
Return to the roundabout and go straight over this time, following signs to the outskirts of **Siggiewi** (✝🖼; Walks 18 and 19). The agro-tourism 'Limestone Heritage' attraction★ on the village outskirts is interesting. Bear left around this town, following signposting for Rabat, and turn off left at a crossroads (where a poorly-surfaced road from Zebbug comes in from the right). This roughly-surfaced road leads up the Girgenti Valley, twice crossing the route of Walk 16, and emerges at the impressive vertical Dingli Cliffs (see Walk 14 and photograph on page 84). Turn right past the army post to

Dingli (58km ✝✕), with its distinctive silver-domed church, visible from miles around.
A signposted road on your right, in the centre of the village, leads you to **Verdala Palace** (60km ◼✕; photograph page 92) and the **Buskett Gardens** (*P*16), further settings for Walk 16. The palace, which was once the summer residence of the Grand Masters and is now a government guesthouse for VIPs, is only open very occasionally to visitors, but the gardens are open daily.
From Verdala Palace make for Rabat and then follow signs for Attard and Valletta. The **Ta' Qali Craft Village** and the **National Park★** (signposted on the left) are worth visiting on weekdays. At 67.5km turn off left (signposted Balzan/San Anton) to the **San Anton Gardens** and the President's imposing residence, for a shady stop amongst subtropical plants (Walk 4).
The final stage of the tour re-enters the conurbation and goes through **Birkirkara** and **Msida** to Sliema (74km).

Car tour 3 GOZO: A HIDDEN GEM

Mgarr • Ir-Ramla • Marsalforn • Victoria • Dwejra Bay • Xlendi • Mgarr

40km/25mi; about 1h45min driving

On route: Picnics (**P** symbol; see pages 9-14): 24a, 24b, 26e; Walks 23-26. (Picnics 23a, 23b, 25 and 26a-c are not far off the

touring route.)

A gentle little tour on roads of variable, but generally reasonable quality, this circuit includes most of Gozo's highlights.

A visit to Gozo is usually regarded as the highlight of a holiday in the Maltese Islands. It is less urbanised, and its greater dependence on agricultural activities make it ideal for touring. The landscape is characterised by flat-topped hills that seem to rise out of terraced fields, and a dozen or so small villages each dominated by a honey-coloured church.

The tour starts and ends at Mgarr, on the assumption that most visitors will come over on the ferry from Malta. (Walks 25 and 26 also start here). On arrival at pretty **Mgarr** harbour (✖🍴), it is better to let the crowds disperse rather than join the convoy of vehicles up the hill. Taking some leisurely refreshment at one of the quaint waterside bars allows one to appreciate the picturesque little harbour.

Climb uphill on the main road and, at the first bend, turn right towards Qala and Nadur on a narrower road which hugs the cliff-edge. Under one kilometre from the harbour, turn right along Triq Zewwieqa. On reaching the outskirts of **Qala** (2.5km) there is a good viewpoint (📷 with seats) looking out over Comino and northern Malta. Almost immediately, turn left towards the village centre, then turn right on reaching the main road and go left at the *pjazza* and parish church, in the direction of Nadur. (Alternatively, go straight ahead and make a short detour towards the eastern suburbs, to view a large windmill that is

unfortunately not open to the public.) Climb steadily, then bear left at the top of the street into more modern housing, much of it built by returning emigrants who have spent their working lives in Australia, Canada or the USA. Head for the neighbouring village of **Nadur**, which enjoys commanding views from its ridge-top position. Like Qala, Nadur is a typical Gozitan community, with its large church, central square with a few shops and bars, and much new suburban housing.

From Nadur just follow signs to beautiful **Ir-Ramla★** (7.5km 🚻 **P**26e; photograph page 33), a large golden sandy beach visited on Walk 26. Retrace your route from the bay for only a few hundred metres and then branch off on a minor road on the right. At first it follows a watercourse in the Ramla Valley, and in under another kilometre it swings right and then left, climbing towards the southern edge of the sprawling hilltop village of **Xaghra** (10.5km 🏔✖🍴📷). Turn right at the T-junction (but

Mgarr harbour, where the car tour and Walks 25 and 26 begin

bear left if you wish to visit the impressive prehistoric temples of Ggantija, only a few minutes away, in a fenced enclosure; **↟**) and then proceed more or less straight through Xaghra to **Marsalforn** (13km ▲ ✕ 🖵 🖾), an old fishing town which is now a popular resort. Take the main road up the valley to **Victoria**, the capital (▲ ✕ 🖵 ✚ ⊕ 🖾 M), which is well worth exploring. Walks 23 and 24 radiate from Victoria, and Walk 25 ends here.

On reaching the main street in the centre of Victoria (Triq ir-Repubblika) turn right, passing the citadel on higher ground on the right; then follow signs for San Lawrenz and Dwejra. At just over 19km a detour of about 3km may be taken, to the isolated church of Ta' Pinu (✚), famous for its miracles: take the road on the right towards Ghammar. The quaint little village of Gharb (Walk 23) is also worth a visit on this diversion; it has an attractive

church, a folk museum, and a timeless village square. When you regain the main road, turn right to San Lawrenz.

At **San Lawrenz** the road forks left to **Dwejra Bay** (*P*24b) and the **Inland Sea**★ (22.5km 🖾). The descent to Gozo's most remote corner is quite barren and spectacular. Here you will find the rock arch shown on page 115, magnificent vertical cliffs, Fungus Rock (see overleaf), and a large, shallow enclosed pool which is perfect for swimming. This is one of the settings for Walk 24.

The only realistic way to get back to Victoria is to retrace your outward route. On reaching the outskirts of Victoria (just past the isolated Gelmus Hill on the left), fork right (signposted Kercem/Santa Lucija) and follow the signs to Xlendi, passing the Knights' wash-house★. The road winds its way down a narrow ravine to the little fishing village at the bottom. **Xlendi**★ (31.5km ▲ ✕

25

☞*P*24a), with its pastel-coloured houses sheltering at the end of a fjord, is one of the most picturesque places in the Maltese Islands. It is also a very popular lunch venue with tourists. Some two-storey housing on the waterfront has been replaced by taller buildings. The bay is still delightful for swimming, and if you fancy a picnic, you can find quiet seats on the esplanade that leads towards Xlendi Tower. (Walk 24 passes through here.)

Return to Victoria and, this time, turn right at Pjazza San Frangisk for the return ferry from Mgarr. Xewkija Dome, which may be larger than Mosta Dome, is the most striking feature of the return trip. For another good viewpoint over the harbour, turn right by the church along Triq Lourdes, just before the final descent to the quayside in Mgarr (40km).

Wild hyacinths near Qala (top) and the Knights' wash-house, on the way to Xlendi

Fungus Rock, one of Gozo's landmarks, is all that remains of the rock wall which once enclosed Dwejra Bay (Picnic 24b)

☀ *Walking*

The Maltese Islands may appear small compared with other Mediterranean islands. A glance at a map also suggests that Malta is densely populated; however you'll be surprised and delighted to find varied scenery and many hidden places in the countryside. Gozo, with its slower pace of life, is a walkers' paradise — a richly cultivated landscape overlooked by hilltop villages. The cliff scenery on both Malta and Gozo is breathtaking, while tiny Comino offers tranquillity and some fine views.

The walks in this book are intended as day excursions that are accessible by public transport and should give you an excellent cross-section of land- and seascapes on all three islands. Obviously there are many other walking possibilities, but access by public transport might be a problem. If you have a car at your disposal, you can use the maps to create your own walk combinations.

There are walks in this book for everyone.

Beginners can start on the walks graded 'easy': be sure to check all the short and alternative walks — some are easy versions of the longer hikes. You need look no further than the picnic suggestions on pages 9 to 14, to find a large selection of gentle strolls, many on level ground. The town walks are fairly short and, apart from some steps in Walks 1 and 2, are on flat ground. Otherwise, I particularly recommend Walks 4, 9, 19 and 22.

Experienced walkers: If you are accustomed to rough terrain you should be able to enjoy all the walks in this book. But note that a couple of the hikes demand a head for heights. Take into account the season and weather conditions, too. Don't attempt the more strenuous walks in high summer. Always remember that heavy rainfall could make any walk described in this book unsafe! If you have not come to one of the landmarks after a reasonable time, please go back to the last sure point and start again.

Experts: There are few walks to challenge you, so relax and enjoy the exhilarating scenery and fascinating history.

Waymarking and maps

Signposting of walks has only recently begun on the islands. Tracks and footpaths abound in areas that are intensively cultivated, but many peter out in fields.

Walk 12: view downstream over the Chadwick Lakes, from the bridge crossed 15 minutes into the walk

The routes described in this book have been over-printed on 1:25,000 **maps** published in 2009/2010 by the Planning Authority in Floriana. (To save space, we have reduced the maps to a scale of 1:32,000.) These new maps are divided into two sheets, a very large sheet covering just Malta and a more manageable sheet for Gozo and Comino; both can be purchased in Malta or from your usual map supplier. The maps are **GPS compatible:** UTM (33S) projection, Datum European 1950. But the handiest and most economical one-sheet map is Kompass map 235 Malta/Gozo at a scale of 1:25,000.

Walkers'checklist
The following points cannot be stressed too often:
- **Never walk alone**. Four is the best walking group: if someone is injured, two people can seek help, so there will be no need to panic in an emergency.
- **Do not overestimate your energies.** Your speed will be determined by the slowest walker in your group.
- **If a walk becomes unsafe**, do not try to press ahead.
- **Transport connections** at the end of a walk are very important.
- **Proper shoes** or boots are vital.
- Always take a **sunhat** with you, and in summer a cover-up for your arms and legs as well.
- **Warm clothing** is needed on the ridges and coasts, especially in windy weather and after sundown. Even in summer, take it along, in case you are delayed.
- Carry **water and food** with you, especially on the longer walks.
- **Compass, whistle, torch, first-aid kit and mobile phone** weigh little, but could save your life.
- A **stout stick** is a help on rough terrain and to discourage the rare unfriendly dog.
- Read and re-read the **Important note** on page 2 and the **Country code** on page 34, as well as guidelines on grade and equipment for each walk you plan to do.

What to take

If you are already on Malta when you find this book, and you do not have items like a rucksack, you can still enjoy a number of the easier walks, or you can buy some equipment in one of the sports shops. Please do not attempt the longer or more difficult walks without the proper equipment. For each walk described, the absolute *minimum* equipment is given. Do modify the equipment according to the season: for instance, carry a long-sleeved shirt and long trousers as well as a sunhat in summer, and put them on before noon to avoid sunburn; take cardigans and raingear on cooler days. Above all, you need thick-soled stout shoes or walking boots which provide good ankle support. The often stony and dusty tracks on the islands can be unforgiving towards the improperly-shod walker.

Please bear in mind that I have not done *all* the walks in this book under *all* weather conditions. I may not realise just how hot or how wet a walk can be in certain seasons. Be particularly vigilant when there is a cool breeze: you can still get sunburn or sunstroke.

If you intend going to Malta properly kitted-out, you may find the following checklist useful:

stout shoes or walking boots
  (broken-in and comfortable)
long trousers, tight at the ankles
waterproof clothing
  (outside summer months)
first-aid kit (bandages, plasters
  etc)
torch (if only for inspecting
  the darkened interiors of
  small chapels…)
long-sleeved shirt
  (for sun protection)
'Dog Dazer' (see page 32)
up-to-date bus and ferry
  timetables (see page 8)

small/medium-sized rucksack
knives and openers
lightweight jacket
whistle, compass
string, clips, safety pins
sunhat
extra bootlaces
plastic rainhat
plastic cups, plates
2 light cardigans
extra pairs of socks
plastic groundsheet
protective sun cream
telephone numbers of
  taxi operators

I rely on your good judgement to modify our equipment according to circumstances and the season.

Weather

The climate is typically Mediterranean, with long hot summer days and mild winters.

Rainfall is mainly confined to the months September to April and, even then, there are relatively few days when the sun does not shine.

Strong **winds** are a feature of the climate: these help to moderate the high summer temperatures, but bear in mind that they add to the chill factor in winter, especially if you are walking on the ridges or the cliffs. Always carry warm clothing with you in the winter months; wind chill is always a possible risk in exposed locations.

The **best months for walking** are from March to May, when the countryside is a riot of wild flowers and the crisp northwesterly winds ensure superb visibility. October and November are also good months for hiking.

If you walk in winter, note that after heavy rain some of the crossings over normally-dry *wieds* (valleys) may be difficult, and the cliff paths can be exceedingly slippery and potentially hazardous.

AVERAGE TEMPERATURES AND RAINFALL

month	average air temperature minimum °C	°F	maximum °C	°F	average sea temperature °C	°F	average hours of sun	average rainfall in mm
Jan	9.5	49	15.0	59	14.5	58	5.3	88.2
Feb	9.4	49	15.4	60	14.5	58	6.3	61.4
Mar	10.2	50	16.7	62	14.5	58	7.3	44.0
Apr	11.8	53	18.7	65.5	16.1	61	8.3	27.5
May	14.9	59	23.0	73.5	18.4	65	10.0	9.7
Jun	18.6	65.5	27.4	81.5	21.1	70	11.2	3.4
Jul	21.0	70	30.2	86.5	24.5	76	12.1	0.9
Aug	21.8	71	30.6	87	25.6	78	11.3	9.3
Sep	20.2	68.5	27.7	82	25.0	77	8.9	44.4
Oct	17.1	63	23.7	75.5	22.2	72	7.3	117.9
Nov	13.8	57	19.9	68	19.5	67	6.3	75.5
Dec	11.1	52	16.7	62	16.7	62	5.2	96.0

Photography

Photography is forbidden in military areas, but you will encounter only a few Armed Forces posts on the walks. Some museums and churches do not allow you to take photographs of the interior; if you are in doubt, ask.

Where to stay

If your chief interest is a walking holiday on Malta, it would be best to stay in the north, particularly **Mellieha** or **Bugibba**. You will have a wide choice of walks nearby, accessible after just a short bus ride. The Gozo ferry is also within easy reach. There are several large hotels in this area, and a wide range of accommodation in Bugibba/Qawra. There is also interesting walking near **Rabat** in the west. However, the greatest concentration of accommodation is centred in the **Sliema/St Julian's** area — a little far from some walks, but the excellent bus service on this small island soon takes you into the field.

For a really relaxing time, away from the pace of twentieth-century life, **Gozo** has several excellent hotels and more modest guest houses. The low hills, rich agricultural valleys and dramatic scenery are a rewarding backdrop for walkers, and the good ferry service means that visits to northern Malta are well within reach, while Comino is just a stone's throw away.

An ideal contrast would be to spend a week in Sliema and another tucked away in an enchanting village on Gozo. That way you could enjoy some of Malta's highlights — and the tranquility of the Gozitan countryside.

The Malta Tourism Authority publishes an accommodation list which includes hotels, tourist villages, aparthotels, guest houses and hostels.

Maltese pronunciation and place names

In Malta, the co-official languages are Maltese and English. English is spoken by approximately 90% of the population. Italian, French and German are also quite widely understood. But since accession to the European Union, the newly formed National Council for the Maltese Language is encouraging greater awareness of the local language. One result is the greater use of Maltese place names rather than their English counterparts. This can be seen on the Arriva bus website, for example, where the destination of BUS 91 from Valletta is shown as San Tumas (St Thomas). *This book uses the more familiar English place names,* but the index includes their Maltese equivalents — for example Cospicua (Bormla).

Obviously it is not necessary to know any Maltese when asking directions or buying bus tickets, but it *is* helpful to be able to pronounce place names.

Maltese alphabet and vowel sounds

Ħħ	The double barred Ħ is hard, the nearest English equivalent being h as in *house*, but in Maltese it is very strongly aspirated, thus Mellie-**ha** (Mellieħa).
GĦ, għ	is silent: **Ine**-sielem (Għajnsielem)
Ċċ, Ġġ, Żż	A dot over these consonants indicates a softening in pronunciation, thus **Ch**-irkewwa (Ċirkewwa).
Jj	is pronounced as y.
Qq	is silent, but may be pronounced as k in rural dialects.
Xx	sounds like sh, thus **Sh**-lendi (Xlendi).
Aa	is pronounced as a in fast.
Ee	is pronounced as e in wet.
Ii	is pronounced as ee in eel.
Oo	is pronounced as o in dock.
Uu	is pronounced as oo in loot.
Aj	is pronounced as i in ice.

Some place-name elements

Aħrax rugged	**Marsa** harbour, inlet
Baħar sea, bay	**Misraħ** wide-open space
Bir well	**Nadur** look-out point
Blata rock	**Qala** bay, inlet
Borġ tower	**Qortin** promontory
Ġebel rocky hill	**Pjazza** square
Għajn spring	**Ramla** sandy beach
Għar cave	**Ras** headland
Ġnien orchard, garden	**Rdum** cliff
Ħal village	**Triq/trieq** street/road
Kbir large, great	**Wied** valley
	Xagħra rocky plateau

Prefixes to place names
il-, iċ-, id-, in-, ir-, is-, it-, ix-, iż- *the*
ta' *of*
taċ-, tad-, tal-, tan-, tar-, tas-, tat-, tax-, taż- *of the*

Examples:
Għajn Tuffieħa *the spring of the apples*
Wied il-Busbies *valley of fennel*
Għar Dalam *the cave of darkness*
Ġnien tal-Isqof *the little garden near the bishop's vale*
It-Tieqa *the window (Dwejra, Gozo)*

NB: With the exception of street names, Maltese spellings are not used in the text, lest they slow up your reading, but they *are* used on the *walking* maps and in the index.

N uisances and hazards

Be aware that **shooters** and **trappers** are about, particularly at weekends·and holidays (see box opposite). Cliff-tops and much of the open countryside are reserved for bird-shooting. Most hunters are friendly and don't seem to mind walkers disturbing them; inevitably there are exceptions. *All hides are best approached with caution and passed by quickly and quietly.*

Most **dogs** are chained, but I mention the (very few) places where they might be a problem. Information about ultrasonic 'Dog Dazers' can be obtained from Sunflower Books, who sell them.

Although you could encounter fairly large black **snakes** on Gozo and Comino, they are not poisonous.

Throughout the Maltese Islands there are many old military buildings and watchtowers. While these add interest to the walks in this book and can be useful landmarks for walkers, some small **gun emplacements** are hazardous and are best not entered. Larger structures, such as forts which are not yet open to the public, should not be explored.

Ir-Ramla (The Beach; Picnic 26e) is best viewed from a group of farmhouses on the edge of the cliff (Walk 26).

Shooting and trapping

If you have not visited the Maltese Islands before, be warned that when you are out walking, you may be distressed by the **shooting and trapping of birds** — a controversial tradition which does little to endear the islands to visitors.

Letters are often written to the Ministry of Tourism, and several have also appeared in the European press, commenting on the slaughter of so many migratory birds.

Yet this activity is perfectly legal and, indeed, has long historical roots. The Knights, for example, deliberately planted trees to create environments in which the shooting of birds took place. Today this pastime is carried on by several thousand Maltese men, usually in cliff-top areas and in the more hilly parts of Malta and Gozo.

Some hunters and bird-trappers are friendly and do not go out of their way to object to the presence of walkers in the vicinity. Others are less comfortable about sharing the countryside with people who are simply there to enjoy the scenery, and evidence of this can be seen in the various 'keep out' and 'private' signs, as well as gates, fences and various other barriers that have mushroomed in some parts of Malta in recent years.

There are two kinds of activity which you will notice at some points on almost all the walks. Firstly, **small shooting hides** which are best passed by quickly and quietly. Sometimes you will also see small cages on rock pillars, containing decoy sparrows and chaffinches. Secondly, hides are sometimes associated with areas of ground that have been cleared of loose stones and on which **nets and wires** have been laid to trap birds. These devices are quite small-scale (measuring no more than 15-20m/yds by 4-5m/yds and are mainly found in cliff-top areas.

If shooting is taking place close by, *additional caution is required,* and it is best not to look skywards just in case spent cartridge shot is falling. It is worth wearing *sunglasses* if you do find yourself in an area where shooting is occurring. *Bright-coloured clothing* will also make your presence visible to shooters. Avoid colours such as green, brown and grey, as these blend into the landscape too easily.

Malta, Gozo and Comino have extensive areas of high cliffs, as well as some rocky under-cliff areas. Keep a safe distance from the **cliff-edge**. After wet weather the descent on the clay slopes beyond Fort Campbell (Walk 7) can be hazardous. On Walk 26 a 'short cut' through the Mistra Rocks between Dahlet Qorrot and San Blas Bay is *very dangerous* and must not be attempted.

Country code for walkers and motorists

The experienced rambler is accustomed to following a 'country code' on his walks, but the tourist out for a lark can unwittingly cause damage, harm animals and even endanger his own life. A code of behaviour is important wherever people are free to roam over the countryside, and doubly so on rugged terrain. On the Maltese islands, special care should be taken to avoid fires.

- **Do not light fires** or allow children to play with matches. Never throw cigarette ends away in woodland. If you see a fire in or near woodland, use the nearest telephone to inform the police.
- **Do not frighten animals.** By making loud noises or trying to touch or photograph them, you may cause them to run in fear and be hurt.
- **Do not leave gates open**, unless that is how you find them. Although animals may not be in evidence, the gates do have a purpose; generally they keep grazing or herded sheep or goats in (or out of) an area.
- **Do not pick wild or cultivated plants.** Leave them in place for others to enjoy. Flowers would die before you got them back to your hotel, and fruit is obviously someone's livelihood.
- **Do not pollute the countryside with your litter.**
- **Do not block roads or tracks** when out driving. Park where you will not inconvenience anyone or cause danger.
- **Do not take risks while out walking.** Don't attempt walks beyond your capacity. Remember that there is very little twilight on Malta. If you were to injure yourself, it might be a very long time before you were found. Do *not* walk alone, and *always* tell someone responsible — perhaps at the hotel desk — exactly where you are going and what time you plan to return. On any but a very short walk near villages, be sure to carry a first-aid kit, whistle, torch, an extra woolly and plenty of water. It's a good idea to take along some high-energy food like chocolate, too.

Organisation of the walks

Each of the 27 rambles in this book was chosen for its accessibility from the main tourist resorts. They fall into six groups: town walks, northern Malta around Mellieha and Bugibba; western Malta, centred on Rabat, Dingli and Siggiewi; southeastern Malta, with Marsaxlokk and Marsascala as the focal points; Gozo; and Comino. The small size of the islands and the efficient public bus system will ensure that there are several walks near your resort, and many others only a short trip away.

The book is set out so that the walks can be planned easily. You might begin by looking at the touring map inside the back cover. Here you can see at a glance the overall terrain, the road network, and the orientation of the individual walking maps in the text. Quickly flipping through the text, you'll also find that there's at least one photograph for each walk.

Having selected one or two potential excursions from the map and photographs, look over the planning information at the beginning of each walk: distance/time, grade, equipment and how to get there. There are almost always short and alternative versions of the main walk; if even these seem like too much effort, turn to the picnic suggestions for gentle after-lunch strolls. Alternatively, the energetic can use the notes and maps to combine the walks and make long hikes.

When you are on your walk, you will find that the text begins with an introduction to the overall landscape and then quickly turns to a detailed description of the route itself. The **maps** (all reproduced at a scale of 1:32,000) show key landmarks. **Times** are given for reaching many of these landmarks. Timing depends on many factors but, once you've done one walk, you'll be able to compare my times with your own pace. Note that the times given *do not include any stops!* Allow extra time for picnics, photography and the like.

Below is a **key to the symbols** on the walking maps:

▬▬▬	trunk road	🚌 🚏	bus stop.best views
▬▬	other main road	Ch.Cha.Sch	church.chapel.school
▬	local road	Hosp.Pol Sta	hospital.police station
═══	minor access road, lane	Bks.Cem	barracks.cemetery
▪▪▪▪▪	tunnel	✝ Tower	antiquity (tower, palace, etc)
‑‑‑‑‑	track/footpath	▪ ▪ Resr ○	water tank.reservoir.spring
2 →	walking route and direction	🏳 ☐	quarry.specific building
2 →	alternative route	P 🚗	picnic spot and nearby car
— 40 —	height (in metres)		parking (see pages 9-14)

Walk 1 MALTA: VALLETTA — CAPITAL AND PLANNED TOWN

Distance: 3.7km/2.3mi; about 1h
Grade: quite easy, but there is a steepish ascent from the War Museum back to the centre, and another on the optional detour to Victoria Gate

Equipment: comfortable walking shoes, sunhat
How to get there and return: 🚌 to City Gate (Valletta bus terminus)

Valletta was planned as a fortified town shortly after the Turks withdrew following their unsuccessful Great Siege of Malta in 1565. The town occupies much of the Sciberras Peninsula, on ground that is higher than the Three Cities (Walk 2) which lie on the south side of the Grand Harbour. Laid out on a grid plan designed by the Italian architect Francesco Laparelli, Valletta was named after the Grand Master of the Knights of St John, Jean de La Vallette. Impressive fortifications, fine public buildings and the legacy of strict planning regulations are among the features which make this walk memorable. But unfortunately, streets laid out in the 16th century are not ideal for vehicle access to business premises: while much of the main shopping street (Triq Ir-Repubblika) has been pedestrianised, on some of the other narrow streets your progress will be impeded by vehicles parked on the pavements.

To **start out**, enter the **City Gate**. Until it is completed in 2013, you will immediately pass a redevelopment site — the Royal Opera House, destroyed in a bombing raid during World War II. Take the first right just beyond the building site (Triq Nofs-in-Nhar) and you will arrive at Castille Place, overlooked by the beautiful green-shuttered **Auberge de Castille et Leon**, now the Prime Minister's office. Continue straight ahead (the old Garrison Church, which has been converted into the Stock Exchange, is on your right) and enter the **Upper Barracca Gardens**, where the stunning views of the Grand Harbour, the Three Cities and the dockyard must be among the most photographed scenes in Malta.

Walk back to the entrance of the gardens and turn right into Triq Sant' Ursula. In 60m/yds turn right again, then almost immediately left into Triq Il-Batterija.

Just beyond the British Hotel there is a small café with tables in the open air overlooking the Victoria Gate, the quayside entrance to the city. In this area you have a first look at the very tall tenement houses, many with distinctive balconies, and the clever way in which streets and steps have been planned to accommodate the steeply-sloping ground. Pause for a moment at the FOOTBRIDGE OVER Triq Il-Lvant or, better still, take a 15-minute detour down some steps, to see the beautifully-restored Victoria Gate and the wharves near the old fish market.

Resuming the main walk, St Barbara Bastion with its shady trees overlooking the harbour gives way to Triq Mediterran and more pleasant greenery, the **Lower Barracca Gardens**, where there is a kiosk. From here the walk turns northeast, passing the **Mediterranean Conference Centre** (formerly the Sacra Infermeria of the Knights of St John) and **Fort St Elmo**, the scene of heroic resistance against the Turkish forces during the Great Siege. Just beyond the main fort entrance is the **National War Museum**, containing relics of the battle for Malta during World War II. The next building of interest is the **Auberge de Bavière**, the former residence of the Bavarian Knights, which now houses government departments. The vistas along this stretch are towards Sliema and the old forts and barracks on Manoel Island (closed at time of writing for restoration and redevelopment) and Tigne.

The bastions, seen from the old fish market

VALLETTA

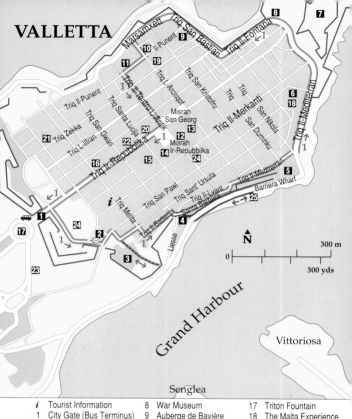

i	Tourist Information	8	War Museum	17	Triton Fountain
1	City Gate (Bus Terminus)	9	Auberge de Bavière	18	The Malta Experience
2	Auberge de Castille	10	Auberge d'Aragón	19	Archbishop's Palace
3	Upper Barracca Gardens	11	St Paul's	20	Theatre
4	Victoria Gate	12	Grandmaster's Palace	21	Fire Arts Museum
5	Lower Barracca Gardens	13	Armoury	22	Law Courts
6	Mediterranean Conference Centre	14	National Library	23	Sunday Morning Market
7	Fort St Elmo	15	St John's (also Museum)	24	Craft Centre
		16	Archaeological Museum	25	Old Fish Market

Pass the **House of Catalunya** and immediately turn left up some steps (Triq L-Arcisqof), to reach a small square (Pjazza Independenza), with the **Auberge d'Aragón** on your left. Then turn right into Triq Il-Punent (where **St Paul's Anglican Pro-Cathedral** is on your right). Take the next left (Triq Il-Tiatru) to reach the main squares in the heart of the city. On the south side of Pjazza San Gorg is the **Grandmaster's Palace**, which is worth visiting to see the state rooms decorated with magnifi-

cent paintings depicting the Great Siege, and the **Armoury**. Proceed west along Triq Ir-Repubblika, past Misrah Ir-Repubblika, a square with several good cafés. It is overlooked by the **Malta National Library** which contains the archives of the Knights. You are now entering the main shopping area; **St John's Co-Cathedral** is off to the left and the **National Museum of Archaeology** is further along on the right. A few minutes walking should see you back at **City Gate**.

38

Walk 2 MALTA: THE THREE CITIES: COSPICUA, SENGLEA AND VITTORIOSA

Distance: 6.4km/4mi; about 1h25min
Grade: easy, with only a few flights of steps. Little shade on the bastions, some shade in Vittoriosa
Equipment: comfortable walking shoes, sunhat, water
How to get there and return: 🚌 2 from Valletta to/from Vittoriosa. Departures every 10min; journey time 20min. Or 🚌 124 from Marsascala; departures hourly; journey time 25min.
Short walk: Cospicua — Senglea (3.2km/2mi; 40min; easy). Shorten the walk by returning from the main square in Senglea (Misrah Papa Benedittu XV; take 🚌 1 back to Valletta.

A dockyard, an industrial estate on the horizon and some of Malta's (indeed the world's) highest urban population densities may seem a less than ideal backdrop for a walk. And the bus journey from Valletta, passing an apparently-endless succession of industrial sites, gives one few clues to the unique character of the communities of Cospicua, Senglea and Vittoriosa on the south bank of the Grand Harbour. But these areas are ideal for strolls in late afternoon (winter) or early evening (summer), when the low sun highlights the dramatic mix of architecture: housing, public buildings, churches and ramparts.

The **best place to start** is the VITTORIOSA BUS TERMINUS. Walk towards the head of **Dockyard Creek** and the centre of **Cospicua**, passing the quayside known as XATT IR-RISQ. The dockyard is on your right; here, in the 16th century, the Knights of St John repaired their galleys. For almost 150 years this was the site of the No 1 Dock of the Naval Dockyard; today it is being transformed into a marina. The road passes local bars, the band club, the church and shops. Some five minutes along, turn right past the dockyard entrance and climb slightly uphill to TRIQ SAN PAWL, where the Suez Canal Bar is on your left.

Another five minutes sees you at the WALLS OF **Senglea**: proceed straight through the arches into the main square (MISRAH PAPA BENEDITTU XV). On the left is the impressive parish church, **Our Lady of Victories**. The original 18th-century church was destroyed during World War II; the present building, with a war memorial in front, dates from the 1950s. Like other waterfront communities in Malta, Senglea suffered a great deal from bombing raids aimed at ships berthed in the adjacent creeks and the dockyard.

Just beyond the church, turn left on TRIQ SAN LAWRENZ, which leads to TRIQ IS-SUR and the western bastions of Senglea. Here you'll see supertankers and other large vessels in the main dockyard. Continue along Triq-is-Sur as far as the junction with TRIQ SAN FILIPPU, then turn right. In a minute you come to the late 17th-century church of **St Philip Neri**, overlooking a small square (PJAZZA FRANCESCO ZAHRA PITTUR 1710-1773). Pass the church and turn left on TRIQ IZ-ZEWG MINI; this leads to a

39

COSPICUA
SENGLEA
VITTORIOSA

N

0 ————— 300 m

————— 300 yds

Kalkara

Vittoriosa

Kalkara Creek

Senglea

French Creek

Dockyard Creek

**Cospicua
(Bormla)**

1 Bus Terminus (Vittoriosa)
2 Our Lady of Victories
3 St Philip Neri
4 Macina Bastion
5 St Lawrence Church and
   Freedom Monument
6 Maritime Museum
7 Fort St Angelo
8 Gate of Provence and Post
   of France
9 Inquisitor's Palace
10 Bus Terminus (route 22 to
   Marsascala)
11 Port of England
12 Port de Allemagne

small GARDEN at the tip of the
peninsula, with fine views of
Valletta, Fort St Angelo in
Vittoriosa and the entrance to
the Grand Harbour. The small
sentry box, known locally as a
gardjola, is worth inspecting —
including the inscriptions that
are a reminder of less secure
times, when maritime
communities needed to be
vigilant against invaders and
pirates.
Leaving the gardens, bear left
down one flight of steps (the
second flight leads to a small
playing field) and turn right
along TRIQ IS-SERENA — a fine
example of a small back street.
Turn left to the quayside, where
there are several open-air bars.
To end the Short walk, turn right
40

into TRIQ SAN LAWRENZ and
return to the main square
(**40min**).
The main walk continues along
the quayside; passing under the
arch in the huge bastion known
as the **Macina**, you regain TRIQ
SAN PAWL. Retrace your steps to
Xatt ir-Risq and walk straight
ahead to **Vittoriosa**'s parish
church of **St Lawrence**. This was
an important place of worship
for the Knights of St John. The
present church dates from the
17th century and is worth
visiting. There are many
impressive paintings in its
chapels and another, behind the
altar, of the town's patron saint.
In front of the church is the
Freedom Monument, built in
1979 to commemorate the

Senglea's church, Our Lady of Victories, from French Creek

embarkation of the last British military forces on HMS London. Every year, on 31 March, there are ceremonies and a regatta to mark this event.

Continue beside the quay, XATT IL-FORN, to the **Maritime Museum** (open daily), housed in the former Naval Bakery. The next landmark is the old Scamp Palace, which has been converted into the Casino de Venezia, and an apartment complex (St Angelo Mansions Block 1) has recently been constructed further along the quayside. Moorings have been built, and the Grand Harbour Marina is already attracting yachts. Two minutes past the museum, go straight ahead over the BRIDGE and walk about 50m/yds along the waterfront (XATT SANT ANGLU), to a point opposite the the ramp up to **Fort St Angelo** (**1h**). At the tip of the Vittoriosa promontory, this fort played a major role in repulsing repeated attacks of the Turkish Armada during the Great Siege of 1565. More recently, it was the Mediterranean headquarters of the British fleet.

The fort is not open to visitors. Retrace your steps to the St Angelo Mansions (**1h02min**) and turn left up a flight of steel steps between it and the adjacent building. Reach a street and turn left, then go right in 30m/yds and take another flight of steps past a small electricity sub-station. You reach the end of TRIQ IL-HABS L-ANTIK. There was once a high-level access to Fort St Angelo at this point, but it has been severed as part of the redevelopment of the water-front. Walk along the street for some 100m/yds, then turn left

onto the eastern bastions of Vittoriosa which overlook **Kalkara Creek**. The route is along TRIQ EMANUEL ATTARD BEZINA and TRIQ IL-MANDRAGG. After climbing two short flights of broad steps, leave the walls by turning right into a small square (**1h10min**).

At the right-hand corner of the square, by a house named Ave Maria, take a very narrow street (TRIQ IL-FOS). In only a few yards/metres you come to a junction where there is a small shop. Turn right into TRIQ HILDA TABONE. Follow it, then turn left into TRIQ IT-TRAMUNTANA and pass the 13th-century **Norman House** on your left before turning right into TRIQ IL-MAJJISTRAL, where the main attraction is the huge **Auberge d'Angleterre.** Turn left to regain TRIQ HILDA TABONE near the **Auberge de France** and reach Vittoriosa's main square (MISRAH IR-REBHA; **1h17min**). Although most of the buildings that overlook the square are modern — due in part to the heavy bombing of this area during World War II — they are still interesting. The Band Club boasts a green balcony, the Labour Party Club has some traditional Maltese balconied windows in bright red livery,

Top: Grand Harbour marina from Xatt il-Forn, Vittoriosa; bottom: Dry Docks complex from Senglea (left), Freedom Monument and St Lawrence Church in Vittoriosa (right)

while the Sala Parrokkaji resembles administrative buildings found in eastern European cities.

The exit from the square is the street furthest to the left (TRIQ IL-MINA L-KBIRA). In two minutes you come to the restored fortifications of the **Gate of Provence**, on your right. There

are superb views of Senglea from the **Post of France** high on the walls, and the complex also includes a permanent photographic exhibition of Vittoriosa.

Retrace your steps back to the street, turn right and find the BUS TERMINUS for Valletta just across the main road (**1h25min**).

Walk 3 MALTA: MDINA AND RABAT

See also photograph page 2
Distance: 3.2km/2mi; 45min-1h
Grade: an easy walk, with plenty of shade in summer
Equipment: comfortable walking shoes, sunhat
How to get there and return:
🚌 51, 52, 53 from Valletta to/from Rabat; alight at the first stop in the town (just after the bus climbs a steep hill). Return from the bus stop in the Pjazza Saqqajja.

Short walk: Mdina
(1.4km/0.9mi; 25min). Follow the main walk to Mdina and, after completing the circuit of the town, return to the bus stop at Pjazza Saqqajja, Rabat.

Mdina is often called 'The Silent City' — something of a misnomer, since it is estimated that four out of every five tourists who come to Malta visit Mdina during their stay. Mdina received its name from the Saracens, who ruled Malta in the 9th century and strengthened the walls and ditches which separate Mdina from the suburb of Rabat. Although Christianity was restored to Malta by the Normans in the 11th century, the subsequent history of Mdina was characterised by neglect, culminating in the arrival of the Knights of St John who preferred to develop defensive settlements around the Grand Harbour. In contrast, Mdina became the home of most of the Maltese nobility, and it is their palaces and houses which give the city much of its appeal to today's visitors. Rabat, by contrast, tends to be overlooked by many tourists, which is a little surprising, as it contains the site where St Paul is said to have preached, as well as many interesting buildings.

The bus climbs a steep hill to enter Rabat. Alight from the bus at the first stop in the town (the bus then continues on a clockwise circuit of the town). **Start out** by heading into Is-SAQQAJJA, on your right. Walk through this square (passing the bus terminus for your return journey), and head for the **Gnien Howard** (gardens) and **Mdina Gate** (photograph page 2), reached in about five minutes. Cross the ditch and walk through the gate, to a small square. Now most visitors continue along the main street (TRIQ VILLEGAIGNON); I recommend a different, quieter route but, if you follow the crowds, it is a ten-minute walk past souvenir shops, cafés and

St Paul's Cathedral to the Pjazza Tas-Sur, where you can pick up the main walk.

My walk heads between Mdina Gate and the bastions. Turn left into TRIQ INGUANEZ and follow it through PJAZZA TAL-MINA TAL-GRIEGI. Turn right into TRIQ L-IMHAZEN (Magazines Street) and almost immediately take the road to **Mina Gharreqin**, from where there are fine views of the countryside — and some architectural curiosities. The old British naval hospital at Mtarfa is on the horizon, and the former terminus (now a restaurant) of a narrow-gauge railway line to Valletta lies in the valley floor. From Mina Gharreqin take TRIQ L-IMHAZEN where, on the left, you will see a long warehouse building which was used to store armaments. Three minutes past here, turn right into TRIQ IL-KARMNU, which leads to the northern end of TRIQ VILLEGAIGNON. Turn left here, to **Pjazza Tas-Sur**. From the bastions there are panoramic views of Mosta and St Paul's Bay and, on a clear day, it is possible to pick out Valletta's churches on the skyline.

To return to Mdina Gate, walk to the eastern end of Pjazza Tas-Sur, pass the Fontanella Tea Garden on your left and follow narrow TRIQ IS-SUR and then TRIQ SANTU ROKKU to **St Paul's Cathedral**, which was rebuilt after a massive earthquake in 1693. Nearby are the **Archbishop's Palace** and **Cathedral Museum**. From the square proceed through a second

1	Mdina Gate	8	St Benedict Convent
2	Gnien Howard	9	Palazzo Vilhena
3	Mina Gharreqin	10	Museum of Roman Antiquities
4	Pjazza Tas-Sur	11	St Paul's Church and Grotto
5	St Paul's Cathedral	12	St Paul's Catacombs
6	Archbishop's Palace		
7	Cathedral Museum		

13	St Agatha's Church and Catacombs
14	National Archives
15	Mdina Dungeons
16	Tower of the Standard
17	Palazzo Falzon
18	Palazzo Santa Sofia

MDINA RABAT

N

0   100   200 m
    100   200 yds

← Mgarr
↖ Mtarfa

St Mary's Bastion
Mdina
De Redin Bastion
Il-Karmnu
Hhazen
Is-Sur
Santu Rokku
Villegaignon
St Paul's Bastion
Iguanez
Triq il-Muzew
San Pawl
Triq Santu Wistin
Lisbtar
Triq Il-Kbira
Triq Il-Vitorja
Triq Bir Ir-Riebu
Cosmana Navarra
San Frangisk.
Nikol Saura
Pjazza Parocca
Il-Kullegg
Il-Kullegg
Sant Agata
Hal Bajjada
Georg Borg Olivier
Ferris
Buskett, Dingli
Inguanez

Attard, Zebbug, Mosta
Is-Saqqajja
Saqqajja Hill
Siggiewi

Rabat

19	Casa del Magistrato
20	Kunsill Citta Notabile
21	Palazzo Gatto Murina
22	Casa Viani
23	Casa Testaferrata
24	Casa Inguanez
25	Corte Capitanale
26	'The Mdina Experience'
27	Bus Terminus (Is-Saqqajja)

St Paul's Cathedral. Like many churches on the island, Mdina's cathedral has two clocks. In this case, the second clock shows the day and month. But in most cases, the second clock has a painted, fixed time — to confuse the Devil.

square (PJAZZA TA L-ARCISQOF) to TRIQ SAN PAWL, passing the **St Benedict Convent** and **Palazzo Vilhena**, once the seat of the 'Universita' (office of local administration), now a natural history museum.

When you arrive back at Mdina Gate, cross the ditch and turn right into Gnien Howard, where there are seats and some shade. Beyond the gardens, at a road junction and car park, you come to the **Museum of Roman Antiquities** (often referred to as the 'Roman Villa'), where the mosaics of a Roman town house and other finds can be seen. The walk now crosses the road into TRIQ SAN PAWL; at this point you should see large signs advertising a bar and a cafeteria. Narrow alleys and typical Maltese balconies now vie for your attention, and there are plenty of bars for refreshments.

Among the landmarks along Triq San Pawl are the L'Isle-Adam Band Club in the Palazzo Xara, which boasts a magnificent curved balcony, and the St Mary of Jesus Friary. Soon you come into PJAZZA PAROCCA, the focal point for streets in Rabat. The square is dominated by **St Paul's Church**; the open area beside it, where St Paul preached his sermons, is crowned by his statue. Pass the entrance to the church and bear left into TRIQ IL-KULLEGG, where a plaque on the wall commemorates Pope John Paul II's visit to Malta in 1990. He had visited Rabat to pray at St Paul's Grotto, where St Paul lived during his stay on the island. A well-signposted route along TRIQ SAN KATALDU and TRIQ SANT'AGATA leads to **St Paul's Catacombs and Museum**. Another historical complex, **St Agatha's Catacombs and Crypt**, is also only a few minutes walk from the PJAZZA PAROCCA.

Return to St Paul's Church and turn right through the pedestrian area, passing an octagonal obelisk commemorating the kindness shown by the Maltese people to St Paul, then turn sharp right into TRIQ COSMANA NAVARRA. (Or take the next right, Triq il-Kbira, if you prefer the hustle and bustle of Rabat's main shopping street.) Triq Cosmana Navarra, a typical narrow street, leads to the **National Archives**.

Turn left at the junction and follow TRIQ L-ISPTAR past the Local Council Offices (at the junction with TRIQ IL-KBIRA). Continue straight on and in under a minute turn right into TRIQ SANTU WISTIN. Proceed through a little square (MISRAH SANTU WISTIN), and the bus terminus in Is-SAQQAJJA is straight ahead (**45min-1h**).

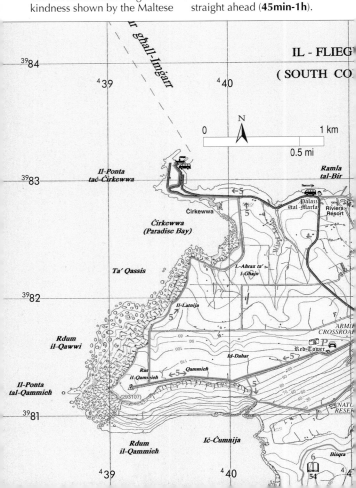

Walk 4 MALTA: GHADIRA • MADONNA STATUE • ARMIER BAY • MARFA

Distance: 10km/6.2mi; 2h30min

Grade: easy, with ascents/descents of 45m/150ft overall

Equipment: stout shoes, sunhat, swimwear, waterproofs, picnic, water

How to get there: 🚐 11, 41 from Valletta (every 30min, journey time about 1h); 🚐 11 from Sliema (every 30min, journey time about 50min); 🚐 11, 41 from Bugibba (every 30min, journey time 25min). Alight at the entrance to the Mellieha Holiday Centre adjacent to the Ghadira police station.

To return: 🚐 11, 41 from Marfa to Valletta

Short walk 1: Ghadira — Madonna statue — Red Tower (6.4km/4mi; 1h40min; easy). Follow the main walk to the statue; return along the ridge road and catch 🚐 11, 41 from the junction near the Red Tower.

Short walk 2: Red Tower — Marfa (3.5km/2.2mi; 55min; easy). Take 🚐 11, 41 to the junction near the Red Tower and follow the ridge road east. Take either the second small road left to Ramla tal-Qortin or the third road left to Armier Bay.

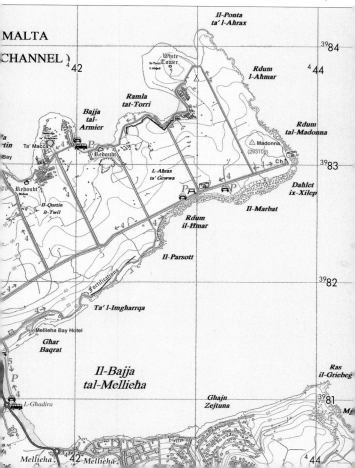

This walk highlights the varied landscapes of the Marfa Ridge, where isolated bays and cliff scenery dominate. The area has also attracted some international hotel chains, and on the northern flanks there is a large concentration of Maltese holiday homes.

Leave the bus on the seaward side of the police station at **Ghadira** and **start out** by walking north along the sandy beach of **Mellieha Bay** (Picnic 4a). At the end of the beach pass in front of the Costa del Sol Restaurant and climb up to the access road leading to the MEL-LIEHA BAY HOTEL. After passing the entrance to hotel reception, reach a pole barrier to prevent vehicle access and walk to the far end of the car park. Take a path that descends steeply

through abandoned terraces, and in two minutes meet the COASTAL PATH (**25min**). Turn left and follow this to **Ta' l-Img-harrqa**; a steep path leads down to this almost enclosed, circular bay, but you continue high above it (**30min**).

Keep parallel with the FORTI-FICATIONS. The coastal path widens out into a clear track, and you come upon the ruins of a jetty; a RED AND WHITE CONCRETE PILLAR stands nearby. Continue on a footpath, making sure that you do not walk too close to the cliff edge; the rocks here are very unstable. At **50min** merge with the ridge road and follow it to the right. A successful afforestation project has resulted in both sides of the road becoming wooded, something of a rarity on Malta, and a chance to enjoy a picnic in the shade (Picnic 4b).

At **1h**, at the top of the hill, a wide panorama opens up, en-

Left: Armier Bay (Picnic 4c); below: holiday homes near Ramla tat-Torri

Looking north along Triq Ix-Xmajjar after leaving the Madonna statue

compassing Comino and Gozo to the left and St Paul's statue just around the headland on the right. At **1h10min**, arrive at an OLD CHAPEL and MADONNA STATUE. Enjoy the fine views, with perhaps the added interest of a cruise ship or supertanker making for port.

Retrace your steps along the ridge road for some 400m/yds, then take a track (TRIQ IX-XMAJJAR) on the right (**1h15min**) leading through walled fields flanked by prickly pear and pine trees. At **1h30min** the track reaches the coast at the MALTA CAMPSITE, where there is a bar. From the campsite proceed straight ahead on a track to **Ramla tat-Torri** (Slug Bay; **1h40min**). (A deviation to the White Tower is not possible, as the access road has 'private' notices.) Continue round the coast, past some holiday homes. You can cut in front of almost all the buildings on the sea side, but in a few places you'll have to follow the wide track behind the buildings. Soon you reach **Armier Bay** (Picnic 4c), in summer a popular holiday area for the Maltese, where you can

sample some restaurants and bars.

Ignoring the road to the crest of the ridge, cut across the headland of **Ta' Macca** (signposted 'RAMLA IL-QORTIN'), past more summer homes, and go on into **Ramla tal-Qortin**. Follow the beach past colourful boathouses and continue in front of the RAMLA BAY RESORT. Bear left past the main building and then right down a lane, to reach a small beach near the old GOZO FERRY HARBOUR at **Marfa** (**2h25min**), now overlooked by the buildings of the RIVIERA RESORT HOTEL. Today boats belonging to diving schools and the ferry to Comino (United Comino Ferries) are the main traffic from the port. A little further on is the PALAZZ TAL-MARFA (**2h30min**) on the main road to Cirkewwa, the present Gozo ferry terminal. Catch the bus at the stop on the corner, next to the Palazz.

Walk 5 MALTA: RED TOWER • QAMMIEH • IC-CUMNIJA • GHADIRA

See map pages 46-47; see also photograph page 52
Distance: 4.3km/2.7mi; 1h25min
Grade: easy, with ascents/descents of 120m/400ft overall
Equipment: stout shoes, sunhat, waterproofs, swimwear, picnic, water
How to get there: 🚌 11, 41 from Valletta (every 30min, journey time about 1h); 🚌 11 from Sliema (every 30min, journey time about 50min); 🚌 11, 41 from Bugibba (every 30min, journey time about 25min). Alight at the junction near the Red Tower.

To return: 🚌 11, 41 from Ghadira to Valletta
Alternative walk: Red Tower — Qammieh — Cirkewwa (4.5km/2.8mi; 1h10min; easy, with an ascent of 70m/225ft and descent of 120m/400ft). Follow the main walk to the old radio station at Qammieh. Retrace your steps for about 100m/yds and look for a concrete pillar on the right-hand side of the road. Take a path on the left just after the pillar and follow it above the cliffs to Paradise Bay. Then take the road to Cirkewwa and catch a bus at the ferry terminus.

This walk is about ridges and valleys, white cliffs, aquamarine sea and Second World War relics. The views from the western end of the Marfa Ridge are among the best on Malta.

The walk begins at a CROSSROADS near the summit of **Marfa Ridge**. **Start out** by taking the small road running west and, after a short climb to the crest of the ridge, pass the 17th-century **Red Tower** (**5min**; Picnic 5) on your right — a historic monument and military post (the varying opening hours are displayed on a noticeboard; there is a small entrance fee). Enjoy the fine views, taking in both the north and east coasts of Malta and extending all the way to Comino and Gozo. At **20min** a honey-coloured wall supporting the edge of a lay-by is visible on the left-hand side of the road; note this landmark for your return. Proceed straight along the road, following the crest of the ridge and enjoying the magnificent scenery and cooling breezes.

At **35min**, above the **Qammieh Cliffs**, lie the remains of a RADIO STATION built by the Americans. From here retrace your route and in 15 minutes (**50min**) come to a path that leads in 20m/yds to a set of rough steps on your right (just after the walled lay-by already described at the 20min-point). The steps lead to a steep footpath with a rather loose surface. It descends past abandoned terraces and comes to a track.

Here turn left, passing the head of the spectacular inlet shown overleaf, **Ic-Cumnija** (The Chimney). At **1h** you reach two small PILLBOXES, from where the track becomes a narrow road leading downhill to a valley of irrigated fields, water tanks, windmills and farmhouses. You'll more than likely see people working their fields or a shepherd herding his flock on the higher ground.

At the junction with the VALLEY ROAD (**1h10min**) turn left towards the coast (by a farm building and a couple of irrigation tanks). In 10 minutes you come to a group of Maltese holiday homes. Turn right and in a few minutes arrive at **Mellieha Bay** — one of Malta's most popular beaches. Cool off and then catch the return bus from one of the bus stops on the promenade at **Ghadira** (**1h25min**).

Western edge of Marfa Ridge, with the Paradise Bay Resort Hotel and Comino in the background

Walk 6 MALTA: GHADIRA • IL PRAJJIET • GHAJN SNUBER • GOLDEN BAY

Distance: 7.2km/4.5mi; 2h20min

Grade: easy initially, then moderate, with some scrambling around Ghajn Snuber and Ras il-Wahx. Overall ascent of 120m/400ft and descent of 100m/325ft.

Equipment: stout shoes, sunhat, swimwear, waterproofs, picnic, water

How to get there: 🚌 11, 41 from Valletta (every 30min, journey time about 1h); 🚌 11 from Sliema (every 30min, journey time about 50min); 🚌 11, 41 from Bugibba (every 30min, journey time 25min). Alight at the entrance to the Mellieha Holiday Centre adjacent to the Ghadira police station.

To return: 🚌 23 from Golden Bay to Valletta

Alternative walk: Ghadira — Ghajn Snuber — Mizieb — Selmun (10km/6.2mi; 3h30min; grade as main walk, with an ascent of 120m/400ft and descent of 60m/200ft). Follow the main walk to Ghajn Snuber tower and walk back to the sharp bend on the Manikata/Mellieha secondary road. Follow the road downhill into the Mizieb Valley. Opposite a group of farm buildings, take a track on the left to Mizieb pumping station. (Now refer to the map on pages 58-59.) In another 5min turn right onto a road; then, in 50m/yds, go left on a track which follows the valley. Continue straight on to the St Paul's Bay/Mellieha road at Selmun. Turn right for bus stops in both directions.

This walk begins and ends near sandy beaches. It also visits the 'Popeye Village', where the old film set and the Children's World theme park are the main attractions. As in Walk 5, you will also come upon ridges, valleys and former military installations.

The walk begins where Walk 5 ends — at the **Ghadira** bus stop. **Start out** by heading inland, past the POLICE STATION on your right and almost immediately come to the main entrance to the MELLIEHA HOLIDAY CENTRE. Go straight on my taking a concrete track (at a sign set in a stone arch, 'Mellieha Holiday Centre'). Follow the track downhill (it acquires a rough surface in 50m/yds), keeping parallel to a prickly pear hedge. In two minutes pass a smallholding and, one minute later, just beyond a wind-pump, bear right through a gap in a wall; and take the right-hand path here. For 100m/yds it runs close to a field wall. Another wind-pump comes into view. Bear left of a farm in the lower ground and follow this path across rocky terrain, aiming for another wall 300m/yds away on the hillside, beyond which there are electricity pylons. There is a gap in the wall close to an ELECTRICITY PYLON with particularly wide steel supports. Go through this gap, then pass to the left of the pylon. Some 150m/yds beyond the pylon, look ahead carefully, and you will see a SOLITARY SHOOTERS' HUT and your ongoing path. The path winds up through a gap between the hill you are standing on and another hill in the distance; it shows up as a distinctive brown colour against the grey/white limestone in this rough terrain. Cross rocky ground to join the PATH (**20min**) and follow it up and out of the valley that so nearly cuts Malta in two.

The top of the ridge is gained in about ten minutes, and you are now on the **Ras in-Niexfa** (Arid Point; **30min**). From here you look out towards the next part of your walk, the Qasam Barani, an isolated and desolate area, which is uninhabited except for the Devil's Farmhouse. Descend from the ridge towards a narrow fjord-like inlet, **Il-Prajjiet** (Anchor Bay; **40min**). Once a lovely secluded spot, this bay was converted into an 18th-century port for the film 'Popeye'. There used to be a lovely cliff-edge path here, but it is now impassable. Instead, you have two alternatives.

The first option is to just walk through the theme park, 'Children's World' (admission is free; the only charges are for the rides and a visit to 'Popeye Village', which is fenced off), then make for the replica church and turn right on a road at the front of the 'church'.

The second option is longer; if you take it, add 15 minutes to all timings. On arriving at the perimeter of the theme park, turn left and follow a low wall on your right for five minutes — until a higher wall comes in from your left. Proceed through a gap in the wall and then join a track leading downhill towards a gate. A path on the right takes you round the gate, then you rejoin the track. Follow the track past a farm and, when you meet the road coming from Ghadira, turn right to reach 'Popeye Village'.

Now for the more difficult part of the walk, where *attention is needed.* Follow the road south round Il-Prajjiet, ignoring the first small road on the left. Keep to the road as it bends left 100m/yds further on, to head

Left: Ic-Cumnija, from the Qammieh Cliffs (Walk 5). Walk 6 follows a route just to the south of the headland in the middle distance.

straight up the gentle north face of **Mellieha Ridge**. At **55min**, immediately after passing a well-camouflaged PILL-BOX, continue straight ahead on a rough concrete-surfaced track. The terraced fields soon give way to the barren slopes of the ridge.

In ten minutes, the track exits at a sharp bend on the MELLIEHA/ MANIKATA ROAD (**1h05min**). Turn right on a lesser track, which leads in a little over five minutes to the **Ghajn Snuber Tower** (**1h10min**). Wild thyme, wolf-bane, rock-samphire, giant hyacinth (*Urginea maritima*), and the late-flowering *Narcissus serotinus* make this setting a real paradise for botanists. Ghajn Snuber ('Spring by the Aleppo Pines') was a military training ground; sadly, the pines have gone.

Walk down towards the cliff-edge, which is reached by following a walled-in track. An old building lies 200m/yds over to your left. A small building at the edge of the cliff is your goal. When you get there, turn left, and after 80m/yds discover a STAIRWAY in the cliff, leading down to two huts with circular walled gardens. The walk now turns south, following the edge of the cliff (but not *too* closely). At the end of the main cliff path, in just under **1h35min**, follow a red earthen track for some 50m/yds, passing to the right of a small stone hut. From the top of the ridge it is easy to see how the rocky headland came by its fearsome name, Horror Point, where a gun emplacement in a dangerous condition is cut into the cliffs (**Ras il-Wahx; 1h45min**).

Return to the cliff-edge, passing a spring which feeds the little plots below. Golden Bay and the old naval rifle range are in the foreground. At the **2h**-point you pass a small ruined war-time FORTIFICATION and a modern walled enclosure on your left. About one minute past here, a track rises from the undercliff on your right (at another disused military building). Bear round to the left, ignoring another track

on the right. Ahead is a large wall (partly collapsed). The track skirts round the left-hand side of this wall and crosses a little valley. In a further two minutes, ignore a track on your right.

You come to a Rural Heritage Project (www.manikatafarmers. com) involving an historic farmstead, Roman tombs, a World War II military post and indigenous trees and plants. In a minute, on entering the outskirts of **Manikata** on a street known as TRIQ MEJJIESA (**2h10min**), walk past new houses for some 300m/yds, then turn right down hill on a dirt track, following telegraph poles. In no more than three minutes, on meeting a road at a WATER TANK AND FARM, turn right. Almost immediately, go straight ahead (the left turn leads across the Pwales Valley), passing a converted farmhouse on the right. Pass the entrance to the OLD MILITARY BASE on your right and in another two minutes, just after another disused military structure, turn right towards the GOLDEN SANDS RESORT and the BUS TERMINUS at **Golden Bay** (Picnic 6b; just over **2h20min**).

'Popeye Village'— the old film set is still a tourist attraction.

Walk 7 MALTA: MELLIEHA • SELMUN PALACE • MGIEBAH VALLEY • BLATA L-BAJDA • MISTRA BAY • XEMXIJA

See also photographs pages 12, 13

Distance: 8.3km/5.2mi; 2h

Grade: quite easy except for the fairy difficult descent after the 45min-point; ascent 145m/475ft; descent 200m/650ft

Equipment: stout shoes, sunhat, swimwear, waterproofs, picnic, water

How to get there: 🚌 11, 41 or X6 to the Mellieha (Belle View) interchange (near the entrance to Mellieha village; see map overleaf); journey time 45min

To return: 🚌 11, 41 or X6 from the outskirts of Xemxija to Valletta

Short walk 1: Selmun Palace — Mgiebah Bay — Selmun Palace (3.2km/2mi; 50min; easy, with an ascent/descent of 100m/350ft). Follow the main walk down the Mgiebah Valley to the bay and return the same way.

Short walk 2: Selmun Palace — Blata l-Bajda — Selmun Palace (4km/2.5mi; 1h; easy, level walking). Take the road from the palace out to Fort Campbell and follow the main walk from the 45min-point to the 1h05min-point; return the same way.

Short walk 3: Selmun Palace — Mistra Bay — Xemxija (1.5km/0.9mi; 45min; easy, with an ascent of 25m/75ft and descent of 90m/300ft). Bear right around Selmun Palace, then turn right on a track. In 50m/yds, turn left on a track/path that heads straight downhill. When you meet the valley road, turn left to Mistra Bay. See page 59 to follow the main walk (either by road or path) to the bus stop outside Xemxija.

The start of this ramble, at a roundabout near a housing estate on the outskirts of Mellieha, may be a little uninspiring! Don't despair; a British fort, a Portuguese redoubt, secret valleys, and delightful coves combine to make this one of Malta's best medium-distance walks.

Set off from the **roundabout** on the St Paul's Bay/Mellieha road in the direction of 'Selmun Palace Hotel'. The road passes through the hamlet of **Selmun** (Picnic 7a), and the baroque-style **Selmun Palace**, bearing the arms of the Monte di Rendenzione, is reached in under a kilometre (0.8km). From the palace tower walk left, following a track that skirts a small farm building. When you come to a crossroads (**15min**), turn right and follow the small road winding down into the **Mgiebah Valley**. This hidden little valley overflows with market garden produce and is one of the last places where the holm oak (*Quercus ilex*), which once covered the islands, still grows. In winter it resounds to the rush of tinkling water in the stone irrigation channels.

On reaching a FARMHOUSE (**25min**), turn right to cross the valley. (Just after turning, a diversion may be made to Mgiebah Bay for Picnic 7b or a swim by following the valley to the sea.) Two minutes past the farm, head right again, following a very narrow path flanked by thorn bushes. You pass another small farm building. Two minutes later, turn left on a small road. This passes through tiny walled-in fields. At about the **31min**-mark, where the road twists to the left, turn right uphill on a path between walls. This widens into a track and in two minutes (**33min**) exits on the road from Selmun Palace to Fort Campbell. Turn left here, in seven minutes reaching **Fort Campbell** (**40min**). This coastal battery was built in 1936. A couple of left turns take you between the old fort buildings (keep the outer wall on your right).

At **45min**, at a sharp left-hand bend in the road, turn right on the lower of two dirt tracks and slither down the clay slopes to the salt pans at **Blata l-Bajda** (**1h**; photograph page 13). The blinding-white rock, indigo sea, and salty spray are exhilarating. Soon a fine viewpoint overlooking the islets of St Paul's, complete with a statue to commemorate the reputed shipwreck of St Paul in 60AD (the statue is more modern), stops you in your tracks. The coastal path takes you to a GUN TOWER and then a manhole access to a cliff LOOKOUT (**1h15min**); *beware here* if you are with children — the manhole cover is missing!

Mistra Valley

Climb more steeply up to **Rdum il-Bies** (Cliffs of the Hawks) and around **Ras il-Mignuna** (Mad Point); then descend to the **Pinto Redoubt** (now a fishery), which stands guard over **Mistra Bay**. This is a fine setting for a swim and Picnic 7c. Follow the road for a final ascent through a valley* rich in agriculture. On meeting the MAIN ROAD (**2h**), turn left for the bus stop on the outskirts of **Xemxija**.

*Alternative end: where the road begins to climb up the valley, turn left on the beach, keeping a group of buildings on your right. In under a minute, take a path/stone steps straight up off the beach. Pass an old quarry on your right (5min) and, two minutes later, bear right towards a walled enclosure. From the enclosure follow the track to a roundabout on the outskirts of Xemxija (12min). Turn left to find bus stops in both directions less than 100m/yds along.

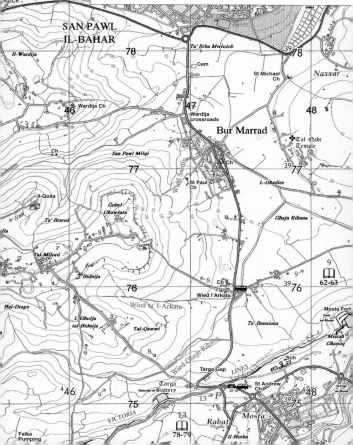

Walk 8 MALTA: WIED L-ARKATA • BIDNIJA • IL-QOLLA • PWALES VALLEY • XEMXIJA

See map pages 58-59
Distance: 9.4km/5.9mi; 2h35min
Grade: easy, with an overall ascent/descent of 190m/625ft
Equipment: stout shoes, sunhat, waterproofs, picnic, water
How to get there: 🚌 31 or 41 from Valletta to Mellieha (departures every 20 minutes; journey time 35 minutes); alight at Wied l-Arkata, the first stop past Targa Gap.
To return: 🚌 11 or 41 from Xemxija to Valletta

Short walk: Wied l-Arkata — Bidnija — Targa Gap (4km/2.5mi; 1h15min; easy, with an ascent of 100m/325ft). Follow the main walk to Bidnija village, turn left just past the church and take the small road back to the main road (it comes out on the hairpin bend at Targa Gap). Return by 🚌 31 or 41 to Valletta from the public garden on outskirts of Mosta — a few minutes east of the hairpin bend.

Inland Malta at its best is explored on this walk, which begins and ends at picturesque chapels. You visit Bronze Age sites, interesting farm buildings and an intimate steep-sided valley. There are panoramic views throughout.

Begin at **Wied l-Arkata**: head in a westerly direction on a narrow road left of the CHAPEL (sign-posted 'TRIQ GHAJN RIHANA'). This becomes a track after 100m/yds. After passing several houses, you gradually climb between fields. After **15min**, where there is a gate into a field, turn left uphill and follow a rocky, overgrown trail up the hill, past abandoned terraces. In five minutes you come onto a road: follow it through the

charming tucked-away village of **Bidnija**, to the church (**35min**). It's very quiet here; there is little traffic, and just one small shop.

Past the church, turn right into TRIQ IL-BDIEWA and, in a few minutes, turn left at a large GATE WITH PILLARS, ignoring the narrow lane that leads into the valley. At just over **40min**, at a restored FARMHOUSE, take the right-hand fork. In a few minutes, turn 90° to the right. Your goal is now the flat-topped circular rock know as **Il-Qolla** (The Fat-Bellied Jug). Engage low gear to negotiate the rough path up to the summit (**50min**), from where there are fine views.

Now retrace your steps to the farmhouse, turn right on an old cart-track and, in a few minutes, turn right again. At about **1h10min** a CLUB-HOUSE FOR CLAY-PIGEON SHOOTERS is reached. Go straight ahead on a narrow earth-surfaced lane which in less than 100m/yds turns 90° to

Bidnija church

Pwales Valley

the left and winds along the cliff-line above a watercourse (the **Wied Qannotta**).

After five minutes you pass a farm on your left: go straight ahead at this point, to avoid the descent into the steepest part of the valley and the climb back up. You pass a house and, one minute later keep straight on along an earthen track, soon coming to the SANTA MARIJA FIREWORKS FACTORY (**1h24min**). A few minutes later, follow the main track round to the right — to the RIDGE ROAD coming from Wardija (**1h30min**), where there are some fine views.

The next section sees some easy walking. Turn left on the road, and turn right on the ST PAUL'S BAY/ZEBBIEH ROAD (**1h37min**). This takes you past a little SHRINE in a grotto, hidden behind gates, where there are seats in the shade. Two minutes later you come to the entrance to the VILLA SAN MARTIN, beyond which you are descending into the **Pwales Valley**. Strolling along, relish the views stretching down to St Paul's Bay.

You meet the ST PAUL'S BAY/

GOLDEN BAY ROAD at **2h10min**. Cross the road and take the MIZIEB ROAD straight ahead, to the hamlet of **L'Imbordin** (**2h20min**). Continue as far as the last house on your left (ANTONIA HOUSE) and go right here on a narrow track flanked by bamboo. In about a minute this becomes a trail between stone walls. In another minute pass a room cut into the rock face and 100m/yds further on come to a small CHAPEL AND TWO STATUES (**2h23min**).

The track twists downhill, acquires a concrete surface, and becomes a minor road passing a succession of farmhouses overlooking the **Pwales Valley**. At around the **2h28min**-mark you come to a junction with farm tracks: turn right and then left (after no more than 60m/yds, at a small WATER SERVICES DEPOT). The road passes the **Is-Simar Nature Reserve** and leads to the outskirts of **Xemxija**. You reach the MAIN ROAD and promenade some 75m/yds south of the PORTO DEL SOL GUEST HOUSE, where there are bus stops for both directions (**2h35min**).

61

Walk 9 MALTA: FALKA • WIED IL-GHAJN RIHANA • GHALLIS TOWER

See also photograph page 61

Distance: 7km/4.4mi; 2h10min

Grade: easy, but there is a rough descent at the start, and some of the cart-tracks are muddy after rain. Ascent 40m/125ft; descent 145m/475ft

Equipment: stout shoes, sunhat, waterproofs, picnic, water

How to get there: 🚌 23 from Valletta to Mgarr/Golden Bay (departures every 30 minutes; journey time about 40 minutes); alight at the stop 100m/yds west of the Ta' Falka pumping station on the Mosta/Mgarr road.

To return: 🚌 11, 12 to Bugibba or St Julian's/Sliema from the

coast road by the Coastline Hotel
Short walk: Falka — Wied l-Arkata (2.4km/1.5mi; 40min; easy, with a descent of 85m/275ft). Follow the main walk from the Falka pumping station to the little stone bridge on the St Paul's Bay/Mosta road (🚌 31, 41).
Alternative walk: Falka — Bidnija — Xemxija (8.8km/

5.5mi; 2h50min; grade as main walk, but an ascent of 130m/425ft and descent of 230m/750ft). Follow the main walk to the ford (20min). Continue straight ahead uphill on a track, to the Mosta/Bidnija road (30min). Turn left into Bidnija and the church shown on page 60 (35min). Now follow Walk 8 from the 35min-point.

O n this easy stroll you will only climb one low hill, and effortlessly take in some of Malta's pleasant rural scenery.

Begin the walk at the TA' FALKA PUMPING STATION, with its large blue-painted gates. Take the small road heading northeast, by a farmhouse. In **5min** turn left on a concreted farm track which leads down to the floor of the **Wied il-Ghajn Rihana (16min)**. Continue straight on (just before a ruined hut and VINEYARD). Four minutes later, ford a stream (**20min**) and immediately turn right on another track, past a small DAM. Meeting another track,

turn right to the MOSTA/BIDNIJA ROAD (**30min**). Cross the road, keeping to the right-hand side of the valley. Shortly afterwards, at another DAM, cross to the left-hand side of the valley, on a narrow path skirting the fields shown overleaf.
A third DAM comes up at **40min**. Turn right and cross over it. A well-trodden path at the edge of a field leads past vines, then rises to another field at a small building with a metal door. From here follow a track for 100m/yds to the busy St Paul's Bay/Mosta road at **Wied l-Arkata (43min)**, where Walk 8 begins. Turn left, taking advantage of the pavement, and after 400m/yds, cross the road and take a minor road on your right (at a large sign, 'MOSTA MERHBA') that runs parallel with the *wied*. In just over **1h** ignore a right turn at IL-BARRIERA farmhouse and almost immediately cross another *wied* (**Il-Ghasel**).
Go straight across the SAN PAWL TAT-TARGA/BUR MARRAD road (**1h10min**) and at a three-way fork keep straight ahead on an old trail between stone walls. This rises to **Il-Qadi** (55m/175ft). After fifteen minutes, at a T-junction by a large new farm

Nearing a bridge over the water-course, on the Mosta/Bidnija road

of minutes later, turn left on a road (by VILLA FREIBUSA), in just over two minutes passing NEG NEG FARM on your right. You are now on the RIDGE TRAIL, heading for the shimmering Mediterranean, with fine views on both sides. The wide fields give way to flat, open, rocky land, the *misrah*. Following a cart-track (a short stretch of which is prone to flooding after heavy rain), you soon overlook Salina Bay. The 17th-century **Ghallis Tower** (built by Grand Master Martin de Redin; **2h10min**) marks the end of the walk. Pick up the bus at the COASTLINE HOTEL 1km in the direction of St Paul's Bay, where there are bus shelters and stops in both directions.

building with wide gates on rollers, turn right on a track (named TRIQ TAL-QADI at the next junction). Emerging on the SAN PAWL TAT-TARGA/ SALINA BAY ROAD, turn right again. A couple

Walk 10 MALTA: ST ANDREW'S • MADLIENA • GHARGHUR • MAGHTAB • BAHAR IC-CAGHAQ

Distance: 7.7km/4.8mi; 1h45min

Grade: generally easy; a moderate ascent to Madliena and another towards Gharghur. Overall ascent/descent of 170m/550ft

Equipment: stout shoes, sunhat, swimwear, waterproofs, picnic, water

How to get there: 🚌 11 or 12 from Valletta to St Andrew's (departures every 5-10 minutes; journey time about 35min); alight at the bus stop about 150m/yds east of the junction with Triq L'Ibrag.

To return: 🚌 11 or 12 from Bahar ic-Caghaq to Bugibba and Sliema

Short walk: St Andrew's — **Gharghur** (5.3km/3.3mi; 1h10min; grade as main walk). Follow the main road to Gharghur and catch 🚌 21 or 23 to Valletta.

This unusual walk begins at traffic lights in the St Andrew's district, on the coastal road to/from St Julian's. Leaving the busy main road, the route goes through one of Malta's most sought-after residential areas, before visiting a peaceful hilltop village with spectacular views.

Start out by walking uphill on TRIQ L'IBRAG, a busy street with many small shops. In **10min** pass the HALLAND HOTEL (now closed). Continue straight on, passing a small fortified TOWER and coming to a T-junction just under three minutes later. Turn

Right: This 16th-century chapel dedicated to the Assumption of Our Lady rises above carefully tended terraces at Gharghur. There are over 300 churches and chapels on Malta, many of the latter in the countryside — built for farmers who were too far from the urban centres for daily prayer.

right into TRIQ MADLIENA (by two houses called ANTONIA and CARO COTTAGE).

After passing two old QUARRIES and a converted farmhouse (SEDONA FARMHOUSE) and two old quarries, your way descends straight ahead into **Madliena** (**25min**). Carry straight on at a wide junction next to the MYSTIQUE NIGHTCLUB and several villas. You pass some fine old country houses near the junction with TRIQ IL-BIR, where you proceed straight ahead. Pass a small CHURCH on the left at the **40min** mark; just beyond it, there are several farmhouses on both sides of the road, some of which have been converted into villas. Just beyond these is a fine view of the Madliena Valley overlooked by Fort Madliena (built by the British in 1880

and still in use by the military).

Ignore the left turn (Triq Wied id-Dis) and, in less than a minute, pass VILLA MADALENA. Then follow a path on the left leading downhill beside a broken-away wall and a line of telegraph poles. The path takes you to an avenue flanked by yet more villas and the BUSIETTA GARDENS APARTMENTS. Continue downhill, turn left at the T-junction, and cross the bridge over the **Wied id-Dis** (**50min**).

Follow the quiet road towards the village of Gharghur. In about 10 minutes you pass a house on the left with a long garden. An inscription in Italian commemorates its housing of the British commanders of the village garrison during the reign of King

George III. Some 100m/yds
further on, you come to a well-
kept chapel built in 1560 and
dedicated to the **Assumption of
Our Lady**. The next landmark,
only another 100m/yds further
along, is a modern house known
as Villa Suzie.

Continue straight on into Triq il-
Gnien and, almost immediately,
turn right into Triq Ghaxqet
l-Ghajn. (If you turn left at Villa
Suzie, then right at the next
junction, this would take you to
Gharghur church and the
village centre, where there are
shops and bars — a detour of
under five minutes each way.)
From Triq Ghaxqet l-Ghajn you
enjoy the fine view of the
Assumption Chapel shown on
pages 66-67. In just under ten
minutes you reach the **Victoria
Lines** (**1h05min**; Picnic 10a),
where there are superb views
stretching from the Maghtab
Plain below to St Paul's Bay,
Comino, and even the dome of
Xewkija's church on Gozo. The
Lines (see photograph opposite)
were built by the British
between 1870 and 1899 on a
high ridge, to protect Valletta
and other towns around the
Grand Harbour from enemy
landings on the north side of the
island.

The Lines are your route for just
under ten minutes, until you
meet a road. There is a small
garden together with seats at
this point (Picnic 10b). Turn
right here (Triq Ghar San
Brinkat) and descend on an
asphalt road to the **Maghtab**
plain (passing a farm on the left).
Continue to a T-junction at a
house called Il-Bejta (**1h35min**)

The Victoria lines, near the end of the walk, were built to protect Valletta and other towns around the Grand Harbour, shown above. At the top is a view to Senglea from the Post of France, below a view to Fort St Angelo (Vittoriosa) from near the Upper Barracca Gardens.

and turn right into TRIQ SANTA KLARA. Pass the VILLA TAL-FANAL and the usually dry watercourse at PARADISE FARM.

At **St John's Church (1h40min)** turn left on TRIQ SAN GWANN EVANGELISTA and in two minutes meet the coast road opposite the **Mediterraneo Water Park** at **Bahar ic-Caghaq (1h45min)**, 68

where there is a bus stop in the direction of Bugibba. The park offers the opportunity to try swimming with dolphins, should you fancy a change from walking! About 150m/yds further towards Bugibba there are bus stops in both directions, as well as a small bar for those in need of refreshment.

Walk 11 MALTA: BINGEMMA GAP • NADUR TOWER • BINGEMMA FORT • L-ISKORVIT • GOLDEN BAY

Distance: 8km/5mi; 2h20min
Grade: very easy, with rougher walking along the cliffs; ascent of 70m/225ft and descent of 240m/775ft
Equipment: stout shoes, sunhat, swimwear, waterproofs, picnic, water
How to get there: 🚌 51 or 53 from Valletta to Rabat (Saqqajja). Departures every 10 minutes; journey time about 35min. Then taxi to Bingemma Gap on the Mgarr road. (Or stay on the bus until the last stop before the Busugrilla round-about in the Nigred Housing Estate in Rabat; journey time about 40min; then walk 2.4km/1.5mi to Bingemma Gap.) Alternatively 🚌 23 to Mgarr. Departures every 30min; journey time 1h10min. Join 🚐 102 to Bingemma hamlet. Departures every 2h; journey time 4min; then walk 1.6km/1mi to Bingemma Gap.
To return: 🚌 23 from Golden Bay to Valletta

Short walk 1: Bingemma Gap — Tas-Santi — Bingemma Gap (7.4km/4.6mi; 1h40min; easy, with an overall ascent/descent of 150m/500ft). 🚌 to/from Bingemma Gap. Follow the main walk through Tas-Santi and, 100m/yds after passing a bus shelter on the left, take the next minor road on the right. Continue for about 10 minutes, then turn left and immediately right (at a stone pillar). In five minutes you reach the hamlet of Bingemma, where a shrine marks your right turn along another minor road — back to Bingemma Gap and your car.
Short walk 2: Mgarr — Golden Bay (4km/2.5mi; 1h; very easy, with a descent of 90m/300ft). From Mgarr Church (🚌 23) go west on the Gnejna road and join the main walk by turning right at the crossroads beyond the house called Zammitello Palace (the 1h25min-point in the main walk).

Western Malta at its best — a Roman cemetery, a British fort, watchtowers, a lovely cultivated valley, and — finally — spectacular coastal scenery to end your ramble.

The Victoria Lines at Bingemma Gap

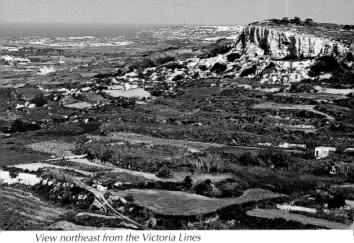

View northeast from the Victoria Lines

Start at the CHAPEL at **Bingemma Gap** (Picnic 11a): facing south (the way you've come): you will see on your left some rock-hewn tombs, reputed to be a ROMAN CEMETERY. Also on this side of the valley are the **Dwejra Lines** (part of the Victoria Lines, setting for Walk 13). Walk south down the quiet narrow road and, in **5min**, turn right at a crossroads. **Nadur Tower** (240m/785ft) is reached in **15min** — one of the highest points on Malta.

From the tower, bear right down a minor road which leads to a farmhouse (**21min**).

Just after passing to the left of the farm, ignore the track continuing downhill; instead take a footpath on your left. The path offers some superb views of northern Malta and Gozo as it follows the **Victoria Lines** to **Bingemma Fort**, which you reach in **30min**. This Victorian fort, which saw action in World War II, retains its original coat of arms and drawbridge. The slopes below may be full of wild asparagus in spring.

Skirt the ditch and drawbridge gate and follow the access road south. Ignore the first right turn (there is a 'no through road' sign on this small road). In three minutes (**33min**) almost opposite a farmhouse, turn right. This narrow road takes you gently downhill. Ignore a small road on the right almost at once (also marked by a 'no through road' sign). This pleasant secondary road drops steadily through the **Tas-Santi Gap**. There are fine views over the terraced fields to the coast and as far north as Gozo.

At **1h05min** pass through the quiet hamlet of **L-Iskorvit**. Cross the MGARR/GNEJNA BAY road (**1h25min**) and, in five minutes (at the top of the rise), take the stony track off left, just beyond a new house with lights either side of a high wrought-iron gate. Zammitello Palace (a country house masquerading as a palace) is perched on the hillside to your right. Soon you're at **Lippija Tower** (**1h45min**; Picnic 11b), standing guard over **Gnejna Bay**. You have breathtaking views across to Il-Pellegrin (The Wanderer). From here take the footpath along the cliff (*not* too close to the edge; rockfalls are frequent in wet weather). You look down on Flat-Rock Bay and the Dinosaur — the peculiar ridge of blue clay, clothed in lilies, that connects the ridge you're walking with Il-Karraba (The Battleship). Where a field wall comes in from the right (**2h**), take a path on the left. This becomes a track, passes some RESERVOIRS and then reaches **Ghajn Tuffieha Bay** (**2h15min**). Walk on to **Golden Bay** and the BUS TERMINUS (**2h20min**).

Walk 12 MALTA: RABAT (BUSUGRILLA) • CHADWICK LAKES • MTAHLEB • IL-QLEJGHA • BAHRIJA • KUNCIZZJONI • MGARR

See also photograph page 28
Distance: 15.2km/9.5mi; 3h50min
Grade: generally easy, but the descents towards Fomm ir-Rih and Gnejna are steep and have been rutted in places by scrambler bikes; sure-footedness and a head for heights are essential. Ascent of 140m/450ft and descent of 300m/1000ft
Equipment: stout shoes, walking stick(s), sunhat, swimwear, waterproofs, picnic, water
How to get there: 🚌 51, 52, 53 from Valletta to Rabat, or 🚌 23 to Mgarr. For full details refer to Walk 11 on page 69.
To return: 🚌 23 from Golden Bay to Valletta
Short walk 1: Rabat (Busugrilla) — Chadwick Lakes — Fiddien Bridge — Rabat (Busugrilla) (3.5km/2.2mi; 45min; easy, with ascent/descent of 60m/200ft). Follow the main walk as far as Fiddien Bridge and return via the 'wet weather route' in reverse (see map).
Short walk 2: Rabat (Busugrilla) — Chadwick Lakes — Fiddien Bridge — Mtahleb — Il-Qlejgha — Bahrija (8km/5mi; 2h; easy, with an ascent/descent of 90m/300ft). Follow the main walk to the centre of Bahrija and catch 🚌 201 to Rabat.
Alternative walk 1: Rabat (Busugrilla) — Chadwick Lakes — Dwejra Lines — Mosta (7.8km/4.9mi; 2h10min; easy,

with an ascent of 60m/200ft and descent of 175m/575ft). Follow the main walk to the Chadwick Lakes and cross the bridge (15min). Then turn right and immediately left, picking up Walk 13 at the 1h10min point. Return as Walk 13.
Alternative walk 2: Rabat (Busugrilla) — Chadwick Lakes — Ghemieri Bridge — Ghemieri — Tas Santi — Mgarr (9.4km/5.9mi; 2h40min; easy, with an ascent of 115m/375ft and descent of 200m/650ft). Follow the main walk to the Chadwick Lakes and cross the bridge (15min). Then turn left and proceed to just before the Rabat/Ghemieri road bridge (40min). Turn right up a track immediately before the bridge, to reach the road, and then turn right. Follow this past the Fiddien booster pumping station. After a gentle climb, take a concrete track on your right to Ghemieri (45min). Go straight through this hamlet, to a T-junction (1h). Turn left at a house called Orangeville. After a few metres/yards, at a shelter where the road bends to the left, take a rough track descending between stone walls. This exits on a road coming from Bingemma Fort (1h05min). Go straight ahead here, then pick up Walk 11 at the 33min-point (almost opposite a farmhouse) and follow it to the end.

S tarting at the outskirts of Rabat, this walk visits the Chadwick Lakes irrigation system and remote hamlets before exploring some of Malta's most spectacular cliff scenery. The closing stretch takes in much of the island's best farmland and one of its least spoilt villages.

The **walk starts** at the BUSUGRILLA ROUNDABOUT in the

Nigred area of **Rabat**. *In fine weather,* follow the road

The Qlejgha Valley near Ghemieri Bridge

towards Mtarfa.* After about **3min**,** where the road bends sharp right, go straight on into TRIQ GUZEPPI GALEA. In a further minute, at the next junction, Wied Qlejgha is signposted; here you take the left-most of three roads (TRIQ TA' SLAMPA); this plunges downhill to the floor of the **Qlejgha Valley**. Cross the bridge over one of the **Chadwick Lakes** (**15min**) and turn left. After about two minutes you pass a retaining wall (to prevent erosion damage). Bear left now, on the lower track beside the *wied*. Pass another BRIDGE AND DAM, beyond which the track merges with the bed of the *wied* (about **22min**). You reach the FINAL DAM a minute later. Steps here take you up to a path running parallel with the increasingly narrow river bed.

Continue by walking under a BRIDGE carrying the RABAT/TAS SALIB/BINGEMMA GAP ROAD. A small tributary joins you from the right (**Wied Ghomor; 30min**). Soon afterwards you pass under the RABAT/GHEMIERI ROAD BRIDGE. There is more reconstruction work ahead,

including a little STEEL FOOT-BRIDGE which looks very out of character with the surrounding landscape — it might even have been 'borrowed' from a harbour or canal. Don't be tempted to cross it to the other bank; instead, continue on the left bank, soon bearing left at a small field and wind-pump, to reach the RABAT/MTAHLEB ROAD at **Fiddien Bridge** (**35min**). Turn right; on the far side of the bridge you come upon a small picnic area and a plaque commerating the inauguration

*In wet weather, follow the signs for Fiddien and you will reach **Fiddien Bridge** in about **10min**. Pick up the main walk at the 35min-point.

**Alternatively, walkers wishing to visit the new town of Mtarfa, where imaginatively restored old buildings associated with the former British naval hospital mingle with new housing, should continue on the main road for a further 50m/yds before turning left. Take the middle of three roads (TRIQ TAL-PALMA; the other roads have no entry signs for

vehicles). Bear right and, after less than 100m/yds, continue along TRIQ L-IMTARFA; follow this for approximately 300m/yds. A belvedere recommended for a picnic can be reached by turning left on TRIQ IL-KONTI F THEUMA CASTELLETTI and left again at its junction with TRIQ SIR PHILIP PULLICINO (Picnic 12a; see map on page 83). Alternatively, continue straight on; the centre of Mtarfa can be reached in about five minutes. To return to the main walk retrace your outward route to the 3min-mark.

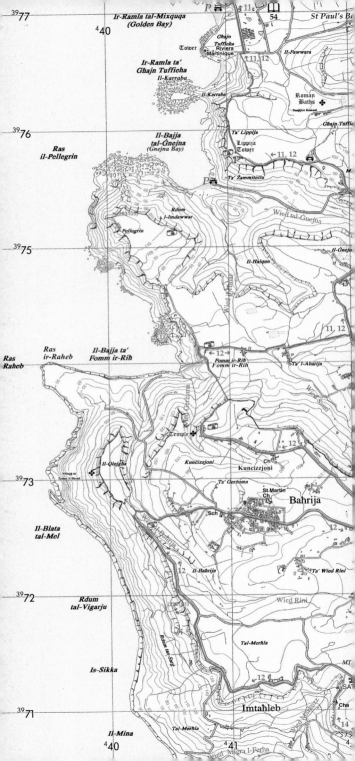

of the project by the Prime Minister on 12 December 1997. So far the walk has been mainly in the intimate confines of one of Malta's deeper river valley systems. The vistas begin to open up as you bear left following a signpost to 'IMTAHLEB' (where the right turn leads to Fiddien Reservoir and Bahrija). Ignore all minor roads right and left, including one to Dingli (and Walk 14) which comes up in about 20 minutes (**55min**).

You arrive at **Mtahleb (1h15min)**, a remote little village comprised of a church perched on the cliff-edge, an abandoned school that has now acquired a new lease of life as a 'SATU' (Substance Abuse Therapeutic Unit), and a couple of houses. Don't take either of the left forks to the church; keep to the high ground. But in two minutes *do* fork left, on a narrow, barely-surfaced road along the plateau. Then bear right a minute later, hugging the cliff-edge. Some 25 minutes from Mtahleb, continue straight on (ignoring the hairpin-bend road down to the coast). Ten minutes later (**1h50min**) you should be gazing at a long oval plateau, the site of a defensive Bronze Age village. In spring the area is a riot of wild flowers, but the spectacular views over northern Malta and Gozo can be enjoyed all year round.

Eventually the road peters out into a track and you turn right on another track, then right again, to descend into the **Wied Rini (2h)**, where the narrow road leading into the small village of Bahrija is visible on the far side. There are many 'private' signs here, but they refer to the fields and huts next to the track, not to the route itself. In just under five minutes you cross the water-course and begin to climb out of the valley. The track meets the beginning of the road leading to Bahrija. A stiff three-minute climb follows. On entering **Bahrija (2h10min)**, continue straight ahead (opposite a house called COUNTRY COTTAGE). Two minutes later ignore a road on the left signposted to Fomm ir-Rih which leads to a car park overlooking the bay. It would be very dangerous to attempt a short-cut from the car park to the main walking route at the 3h10min-point. Turn right at a junction two minutes later. The

BUS STOP, shops and several bars/restaurants in the centre of the village are reached in another minute. This remote community, once quite small, has grown as people escape the more congested areas.

Head out of the village on the main road towards Rabat and, in 15 minutes (just after passing a RADIO MAST; **2h25min**), turn left, back towards the coast (signposted 'Kuncizzjoni'). Ten minutes later you pass the (closed) ALCAZAR GUEST HOUSE, and in a further five minutes you reach the delightful church at **Kuncizzjoni (2h40min)**, where an adjacent gate is inscribed 'Fondazione Paola 1731' — a reference to its founder, Grand Master Antione de Paule. About ten minutes' walking will bring you to the end of the road, where there are magnificent views of Malta's northwestern coastline, with Gozo in the distance.

You have also arrived at the western end of the **Victoria Lines**. Follow a footpath for five minutes and pass a PILL-BOX set into the cliff-face (**2h55min**). Then squeeze into a narrow path that descends steeply some

65m/200ft and follow this until you come to **Fomm ir-Rih Bay (3h10min)**.

The path becomes a farm road for a short distance and passes a large irrigation tank. In about a minute, where it comes close to the cliff-edge overlooking the bay *(protected by a barrier, but keep a safe distance)*, there is a fine view of the headland known as **Ras ir-Raheb**. Turn right into a narrow road at a large farmhouse with boundary walls. The road winds its way through pleasant countryside and several hamlets, the second of which, **Ta' l-Abatija**, should be reached at around the **3h20min**-mark.

From here to Mgarr farming becomes more intensive, and an increasing proportion of crops are grown under plastic. The TAS-SANTI/MGARR ROAD is reached at about **3h27min**, where you turn left (Walk 11 joins here). Follow this for 20 minutes to a crossroads. Walk 11 goes straight on here, heading for the Lippija Tower and Golden Bay. A diversion can be made to Gnejna Bay by turning left (40 minutes return). Otherwise, turn right towards Mgarr with the main point of interest being the Castello Zammitello and its gardens, which boasts two matching conservatories. A further 10 minutes walking via TRIQ IL-KBIRA should be sufficient to reach the magnificent church at **Mgarr** — also known as the 'egg church': built over a long period, it was partly financed by the sale of eggs! There are BUS STOPS in both directions at the junction of TRIQ FISHER AND TRIQ SIR HARRY LUKE in front of the church (**3h50min**).

Mtahleb

Walk 13 MALTA: MOSTA • QLEJGHA VALLEY • CHADWICK LAKES • DWEJRA LINES • MOSTA

See also photograph page 69
Distance: 11.2km/7mi; 3h05min
Grade: moderate, with some rough walking; overall ascent/descent of 115m/375ft
Equipment: stout shoes, sunhat, waterproofs, picnic, water
How to get there: 🚌 21, 23, 31, 41 or X6 from Valletta to Mosta. Departures every 10min; journey time about 25min
To return: 🚌 31 or 41 to Valletta from the public garden at Targa Gap, on outskirts of Mosta
Short walk 1: Chadwick Lakes — Il-Qolla — Chadwick Lakes (4km/2.5mi; 1h; moderate, with an ascent/descent of 55m/175ft). 🚗 Only accessible by car: from the Busugrilla roundabout head northeast on the Mtarfa/Rabat bypass; the lakes are signposted on your left. Drive down the narrow road and turn right to a

dam (limited parking). Follow the main walk from the 1h10min-point up to the road junction and turn right. After 400 metres (a quarter of a mile), turn right, taking a track parallel to the one you climbed up, to go back down to the Chadwick Lakes.
Short walk 2: Chadwick Lakes — Dwejra Lines — Chadwick Lakes (7.2km/4.5mi; 1h50min; moderate, with an ascent/descent of 60m/200ft). Access as Short walk 1 above. This option starts out as Short walk 1 above, but follows the main walk along the Dwejra Lines as far as the fort at the end. From there descend to the lower road and turn right. Come to a track on the left after 1.1km/0.7mi (the 'parallel track' in Short walk 1) and follow this down to the Chadwick Lakes and your car .

This is one of the classic walks on Malta, visiting the longest valley on the island, the famous Chadwick Lakes and the Dwejra Lines. Old forts and barracks provide added interest to a fascinating walk which offers magnificent panoramic views from the centre of the island.

The walk starts at **Mosta Dome**: follow TRIQ IL-KBIRA, passing near to the old Ta' Qali airfield. At **17min**, where the road forks, take the right-hand option (signposted 'MGARR/GOLDEN BAY'), and a few minutes later go right again, crossing the **Ta' L'Isperanza Valley** on an old BRIDGE (**20min**) beside the delightful 18th-century chapel of **San Pawl tal-Qlejgha**. Come to a roundabout and follow

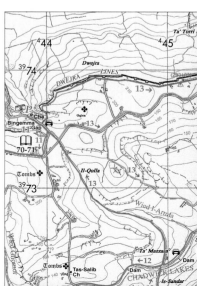

signs for 'RABAT/MDINA', re-crossing the *wied*. Five minutes later, take a minor road on the right signposted 'Chadwick Lakes'. In another five minutes you should again cross the watercourse at the KARBUN BOREHOLE in the **Qlejgha Valley**. The meandering watercourse guides you below the old MTARFA BARRACKS and military hospital (now the site of a new town development), on the hill on your left — aptly named, as Mtarfa means 'Place on the Edge'.

Just as you're about level with Mtarfa, the first of the **Chadwick Lakes** appears (**1h**). Built in 1890 on the advice of Sir Robert Chadwick, to provide irrigation for San Anton Palace, they are quite an oddity in these parched islands. Three minutes later you cross a BRIDGE. In another

minute ignore a gated farm track and bridge on your left. Just past the SECOND DAM and *before* the THIRD BRIDGE (which Walk 12 crosses), take a track on the right (**1h10min**). This becomes a grassy path at an ABANDONED FARM (**1h17min**). Ascend gradually through vineyards, where the hillock shown over-leaf (Il-Qolla) catches the eye. Near the top of the climb, beyond another farmhouse, go straight over a CROSSROADS (**1h35min**). In a few minutes, your track meets another road. Head for the little chapel at **Bingemma Gap** (Walk 11 has already been here), where there are fine views as far as Gozo. Retrace your steps and, after no more than two minutes, opposite a MILESTONE, take a path cut into the rock on the left: this walled path on a viaduct leads

Il-Qolla, north of the Chadwick Lakes

up to the **Dwejra Lines**. It is not hard to see why the lines were built here, as their commanding position affords magnificent views all over the islands. With their gun emplacements, the lines are a military historian's paradise. The former route along the Lines has become overgrown, so follow instead the track to the right.

Towards the end of the lines, at a FORT COMPLEX, descend between the buildings (**2h20min**). In a few minutes the track turns right then left and meets a minor road coming up from the Mgarr/Mosta road. Turn left here, cross the ditch, and where the road begins to turn right downhill, take a track to the left, parallel with the ditch, for no more than 100m/yds. When the track begins to curve sharply away to the left, turn right and follow a track on the left-hand side (northeast) of the Lines. Descend this track — your goal is the road at the bottom of the hill. The track gradually improves and you soon reach

TWO IRRIGATION TANKS. At this point the track swings left, away from the Lines, and passes a farm. You reach the MOSTA/MGARR ROAD in **2h50min**. (Walk 9 begins to your left, at the Falka pumping station.) Turn right on the main road, where there is now a pavement, pass the VALLE VERDE farm on your left and, about two minutes later, turn left at a second farm. The ditch of the Victoria Lines is now your way (unfortunately an unsightly disused quarry is also your companion for part of this stretch), and you come upon several small military buildings, some of which are used for farming. At about **3h05min** the walk ends on the Mosta/ St Paul's Bay road, just above **Targa Gap**. At the bus stop a pleasant surprise awaits you — a public garden with striking views to the coast (Picnic 13). Alternatively, 1.2km along the road would see you back at Mosta Dome.

Walk 14 MALTA: RABAT (BUSUGRILLA) • TAL-LUNZJATA RIDGE • DINGLI • TA' BALDU • TAT-TARGA • RABAT (BUSUGRILLA)

See also photographs on pages 22, 23 and the cover
Distance: 16km/10mi; 3h40min
Grade: easy, with some rocky paths around the coast; overall ascent/descent of 170m/550ft
Equipment: stout shoes, sunhat, waterproofs, water
How to get there and return:
🚌 51, 53 from Valletta to Rabat. Departures every 10-20min; journey time about 40min. The bus does a clockwise circuit of Rabat and will take you to the Busugrilla roundabout in the Nigred Housing Estate, where the walk begins. Reboard at the same bus stop.

Short walk 1: Busugrilla roundabout — Dingli
(6.9km/4.3mi; 1h30min; easy, with an ascent of 90m/300ft and descent of 40m/125ft). Follow the main walk to Dingli and return on 🚌 52.

Short walk 2: Dingli — Dingli Cliffs — Dingli (5.4km/3.4mi; 1h05min; easy, almost level walking). Take 🚌 52 to Dingli and follow the main walk from the village centre to the Coastal Surveillance Post (15min). About 1.5km (1mi) further on, turn right on a narrow tarred road, soon passing some large irrigation tanks and a windmill in the lower ground on your left. In another five minutes, when a narrow road joins from the right, continue straight on. The dome of Dingli church is now in sight. A semi-detached house called Carmel/S Gaetano comes up on your right, as does a final wind-

mill. Five minutes later bear left around the church in Dingli. Continue on to the main Dingli/Rabat road, where there is a shelter for 🚌 52 to the right.

Shorter start to main walk (saves 45min): Alight from 🚌 51 or 53 at the stop for the Ghar Barka Housing Estate (three stops before the alighting point for the main walk). Turn left in 50m/yds on a road signposted 'Santa Katerina, Lunzjata/Ghar Barka Housing Estate'. In about five minutes come to a three-way junction at a house called Madonnina. Bear left here, to 'Santa Rita', a building where the main walk arrives from the lane on your right. Pick up the main walk at the 50min-point.

Alternative walk: Dingli — Ta' Baldu — Mtahleb — Rabat (Busugrilla) (11.5km/7.2mi; 3h10min; grade as main walk, with an ascent of 90m/300ft and descent of 130m/425ft). Take 🚌 52 to Dingli and follow the main walk from Dingli village centre to Ta' Baldu (1h20min). On leaving the hamlet, turn left on a cliff-top path (by some cart ruts). Follow this path to a pig farm, where you keep the first building on your right. Meeting a road a minute later, bear left and follow a track to Mtahleb church. From the church take some steps on your left down to another road, by the 'SATU' (Substance Abuse Therapeutic Unit; formerly Mtahleb School). Turn right and use the map to return to Rabat.

M alta's remote western coastal region, bounded by high vertical cliffs, is the setting for this delightful walk. The ramble also takes in the picturesque hamlet of Santa Katerina set in tranquil countryside.

An old farmhouse on the outskirts of Rabat, possibly dating from 1760

Start off at the **Busugrilla** ROUNDABOUT: follow signs for FIDDIEN. Turn left on the second of two lanes (**5min**) — just 100m/yds after passing to the left of the old farmhouse shown above, with a coat of arms dated 1760. This lane, signposted to Tas-Salvatur, leads uphill to a small hamlet, passing ST JOHN'S FARM in one minute. On reaching **Salvatur** (**9min**), turn left at a farm building (there is a disused wind-pump on the left). A minute later, turn right, and soon go left at a house called ID-DULLURI. *(Beware chained dogs on the left-hand side of the road here.)* In another minute you come to a T-JUNCTION, WHERE THERE IS A DOOR IN A WALL. Turn right here: the small road swings round to the left at yet another farm (QAMMA FARM) and you reach **Tat-Targa Gap** (**16min**).

Turn left on a very narrow road. You may wish to pause for a moment to savour the view of the Fiddien (Silvery) Plain. Ignore the road downhill

through the gap — it will be your return route. Continue south along **Tal-Lunzjata Ridge** past the CHURCH and convent complex, with its hermitage farmhouse and UNDERGROUND CHAPEL (**20min**). Follow the road round to the left. In two minutes continue straight on, ignoring a track to the right. A minute later ignore a small road on your left. After passing a QUARRY entrance, follow the quiet lane uphill; there are GREENHOUSES on your right and the Ghar Barka Housing Estate on the outskirts of Rabat lies beyond the fields on your left. Soon, take a very narrow lane on your right (it is only 30m/yds long). Turn right at a farmhouse

incorporating a shrine on a wall (**30min**). *(The 'Shorter start' joins the main walk here.)* Follow this road downhill through pleasant farmland, where traditional wind-pumps can still be seen at work, and descend into the picture-postcard hamlet of **Santa Katerina**, with its incredible church clinging to the hillside and an ancient farmhouse built into the side of the cliffs. Put your brakes on to negotiate the

sharply descending S-bend as you leave the hamlet. At **45min**, just before a SPRING and a farm on the hillside, turn left along a sandy cart track which winds through an area of intensive farming. The spring flowers add splodges of yellow and blue to the canvas, as they vie for space among the crops. Keep bearing right, climbing past a WELL.

When you come to a fork, where the left-hand turning has

a 'private' sign (**55min**), carry straight on. In three minutes you reach an old farm building close to the edge of Dingli. Bear left around this building and, almost immediately, fork right (by another WELL). In a further two minutes turn left on TRIQ CLAUDETTE AGIUS (1975-1990), at a house called BLANZUNI (**1h05min**). At the end of the street, take some steps between garages, turn left and, a minute later, turn right into TRIQ SALVU AZZOPARDI (1902-1976). In 80m/yds bear left on TRIQ SAN PAWL to the church. From here go left down TRIQ IL-PARROCCA to the main road. You have arrived at the commercial centre of **Dingli** (**1h10min**), where there are shops, a bank, the club/bar of Dingli Swallows Football Club, and a BUS STOP.

The Dingli Cliffs, with Il-Kullana (The Necklace) in the background

Turn right and follow the main road (TRIQ IL-KBIRA) towards the Dingli Cliffs. At DINGLI CEMETERY bear right: the edge of the **Dingli Cliffs** is reached at a COASTAL SURVEILLANCE POST (**1h25min**). Turn right now, and a house called RIDUM DEPIRO on the left (**1h35min**) should provide your next landmark. Carry on along the cliff-edge. The road, which has become a roughly-tarred track at this point, ends at the PULVICH EXPLOSIVES INDUSTRIES factory on your right (**1h50min**). Continue straight ahead downhill on a very rough track which deteriorates into a path. After two minutes cross a track coming up from the undercliff, and after 10m/yds take a path on the right which after 20m/yds meets a track. turn left on the track and pass a SHOOTER'S HUT on your left. The track leads to the left (seaward) side of a field that was reclaimed from the rough landscape by using materials and soil from building sites. Skirt to the left of the field on a path (**1h55min**). Beyond the field, ignore the beginnings of a track on your right. Continue round the cliff-tops, at a safe distance. The northern end of the **Il-Qattara** ridge comes into sight (**2h**), and there are fine views around the wide valley of the Wied ir-Rum and beyond — towards three strange hillocks. If the stream is in flow, a beautiful cascade over the cliff will greet you.

When you come to a group of FARM BUILDINGS, turn right and follow a road along the north-facing slopes of the valley. Then shortly cut off left through a small farm (**2h05min**; ask the farmer for permission, telling him you want to go to Ta' Baldu, *and beware of the chained dogs here*). If you look

back, you'll see the farm has been housed in a complex of Bronze Age caves on the edge of the cliff. The trail descends via hairpin bends into the **Wied ir-Rum**.

It's a steep climb up the far side to the ridge at **Ta' Baldu**, where you encounter a crossroads (**2h30min**). Turn left here, skirt TA' BALDU HOUSE, and then take the old walled cart track. There are fine views to the south, where walled terraces snuggle up to the well-tended orchards. Soon a surfaced road comes underfoot (**2h50min**).

Now we visit ancient Malta, by following this narrow road downhill into a huddle of small buildings perched on the cliff-edge. Sheep and an occasional shepherd are likely to be your only companions here. On leaving the hamlet, follow the road (little more than a track) around to the right and turn right at a T-junction (**3h**). Then turn left in a further ten minutes and go straight ahead two minutes later, past a FARMHOUSE on the right and a vineyard called FRA BRETTEL ESTATE on your left. You are crossing the floor of the plain, and the gap in the cliff-face is your target. This is the road you should have noted in the early part of the walk.

At just under **3h20min** you should be climbing up through **Tat-Targa Gap**. Turning left at the gap, you are now on the road taken earlier. Retrace your steps to the T-junction with the DOOR IN THE WALL on your right. Go straight ahead. At this point Mdina's cathedral is visible on the horizon. You meet the main road at the NIGRED HOUSING ESTATE (**3h40min**): turn right to the BUS STOP.

Walk 15 MALTA: RABAT (TAL-VIRTU) • WIED TA' L-ISQOF • GNIEN IL-KBIR • RABAT (SAQQAJJA)

See map pages 88-89; see also Walk 3
Distance: 4.5km/2.8mi; 1h05min
Grade: easy, with an overall ascent/descent of 60m/200ft
Equipment: stout shoes, sunhat, waterproofs, picnic, water
How to get there: 🚌 51, 52 or 53 from Valletta to Rabat (departures every 10min; journey time 40min); alight at junction of Triq Tal-Virtu and Triq Gorg Borg Olivier. The bus stop is the third in Rabat after the bus has climbed the steep hill into the town.
To return: 🚌 51, 52 or 53 to Valletta, from the terminus at Pjazza Saqqajja (see plan on page 44).

Alternative walk 1: Rabat (Tal-Virtu) — Wied ta' l-Isqof — Siggiewi (5.8km/3.6mi; 1h05min; easy, with a descent of 85m/275ft). This is a very pleasant walk on a summer's evening, when the Rabat/Siggiewi road is quiet and the low sun highlights the terraced fields and distant villages. Follow the main walk to the

wied (21min), then go straight on to the Rabat/Siggiewi road. Follow this to the right. Pass the San Blas chapel (30min) and, ten minutes later, at a complex junction, take the second exit on your left. Bear right at a small stone building (*ignore* the left fork here, signposted to Siggiewi). Pass a memorial (55min) and ignore a small road on the left to Siggiewi. On reaching the outskirts of Siggiewi (1h), bear left (signposted Siggiewi Centre) into Triq Lapsi. In two minutes, where the street narrows, go straight ahead into Triq il-Knisha l-Qadima, to reach the square (photograph page 99) and bus terminus.

Alternative walk 2: Rabat (Tal-Virtu) — Wied ta' l-Isqof — Verdala Palace (4.8km/3mi; 1h; easy, with an ascent of 100m/325ft and a descent of 85m/275ft). Follow Alternative walk 1 to the San Blas chapel. Turn right and in five minutes (35min) Walk 16 comes in from your left. Pick up that walk at the 1h30min-point (see page 91).

I t is often said that Malta remains a deeply religious country, and this little ramble takes you past the Apostolic Nunciature, the Archbishop's Seminary, a convent, an ancient church and — near the end of the walk — the impressive Dominican Church and Monastery, with cloisters dating from the early 17th century. This walk also reveals just how undulating the landscape can be; the walk descends very steeply but, happily, the climb back up to Rabat via the Wied ta' l-Isqof is long and gradual.

The walk begins at TRIQ TAL-VIRTU' in **Rabat**: stroll along this quiet suburban street. Opposite the **Apostolic Nunciature** there is a spectacular viewpoint over the surrounding countryside (**5min**; Picnic 15). This area has been proposed as the site for a

golf course incorporating agricultural terraces. So far nothing has come of the proposal, but savour the landscape while you can! The next landmark comes up in only another minute: the **Archbishop's Seminary** and the

Convent of the Sacred Heart. In a further three minutes, bear right around the high wall enclosing **Tal-Virtu** CHURCH and a fairy-tale CASTLE (**9min**). The tranquil gardens are not open to the public, and there is a 'beware of the dog' sign at the entrance.

The views at this point are now towards the settings for Walk 16 — Verdala Palace, with Laferla Cross visible in the distance. Soon the way becomes a narrow road that plunges down the hillside, so engage low gear. On the higher terraces, there are vineyards and fruit trees; further on, prickly pear 'hedges' and larger trees line the route. Then, on lower ground, the landscape opens out into quite large fields (by Maltese standards). Go straight on past a group of FARM BUILDINGS (**20min**) but, just one minute later, turn right on a small road leading up the **Wied ta' l-Isqof** (there are two small buildings at this junction).

Your route is sandwiched between thick bamboo, which lines the watercourse, and high field walls. Ignore all the side tracks on your left and right. Some 15 minutes along, by a WALL (**35min**), bear left (don't be tempted to take the track that heads uphill towards Rabat; it leads to a private gate). Then turn right almost immediately, still following the watercourse. In a few yards/metres the track swings away to your left towards Dajku Farm, where there are several noisy chained dogs. Now take a path at the right of the watercourse, flanked by yet more bamboo. After 300m/yds, the path widens out into a narrow grass-covered track. When the track turns right uphill at a large prickly pear 'hedge' (**40min**), there are good views of the *wied*.

Five minutes later you pass a large FARM at Gnien il-Kbir *(beware of dogs)*. Turn right almost immediately at a T-junction. On reaching the RABAT/BUSKETT ROAD (**47min**), turn right. There is a BUS STOP for the bus to Buskett and Dingli here, but I suggest you keep on. It's only a 10-minute walk to the Baroque church of **Madonna tal-Ghar** (Our Lady of the Grotto) and the Dominican Monastery. The shady garden outside the church is an ideal place to relax before heading along past your starting point (about **1h**) to the bus terminus at PJAZZA SAQQAJJA reached in a further five minutes (**1h05min**). Walk 3 also ends in this square — and there's no reason why you shouldn't easily combine the two.

Walk 16 MALTA: BUSKETT • GHAR IL-KBIR • LAFERLA CROSS • VERDALA PALACE

See also photograph page 92
Distance: 8.2km/5.1mi; 1h55min
Grade: easy, with some rougher walking up to the cave at Ghar il-Kbir. Ascent of 140m/450ft; descent of 115m/375ft

Equipment: stout shoes, sunhat, waterproofs, picnic, water
How to get there: 🚌 51, 52, 53 from Valletta to Rabat. Departures every 10 minutes; journey time 35min. Change in Rabat to 🚌 107 to Buskett (Dingli/Rabat/Stadium bus). Departures hourly; journey time 15min.
To return: 🚌 107 from next to the Verdala Palace gates to Rabat; change to 🚌 51, 52 or 53 to Valletta

Short walk 1: Buskett Gardens. Several well-established walkways in the gardens offer short, easy walks (Picnic 16).

Short walk 2: Buskett — Wied il-Luq — Verdala Palace (5.8km/3.6mi; 1h20min; easy; ascent of 100m/325ft and descent of 75m/250ft). Follow the main walk for 33min (just past the small quarry),

then turn left on the small road leading to the Girgenti Valley. Follow this down to a bridge over the *wied*, then pick up the main walk again at the 1h15min-point and follow it to the end.

88

This is one of Malta's loveliest walks, with a great deal of charm and something of interest for every rambler. We cover ground more familiar to local people than tourists and visit palaces and cave dwellings … as well as Malta's 'Clapham Junction' (named after London's frenetically busy railway station).

Setting out from the government's GRAPE AND WINE RESEARCH STATION, where the bus stops, turn right (south) immediately past the winery and then left very soon afterwards (signposted GHAR IL-KBIR/CLAPHAM JUNCTION). In **6min** turn right to a CAR PARK. From the car park follow a track for about a minute, to the point where it bends to the left at a field wall. Now a path leads up to a large fallen-in cave (**Ghar il-Kbir; 12min**). Believe it or not, the cave was inhabited until 1835! Close by is 'Clapham Junction' — the name British visitors have given to the large number of prehistoric cart-ruts found in this area.
But back to the cave: retrace

your steps to the car park (**20min**). Turn right downhill on a track. When you approach a wall and gate in two minutes, turn right 15m/yds before the gate (there are some cart ruts here). After 50m/yds pass a shooter's hut and after another 100m/yds, a TELEGRAPH POLE. Some 50m/yds further on, go left, through a GAP IN THE WALL (**25min**). Follow a path which bends left and, in about three minutes, scramble down to a lower level, closer to a *wied* (where you may spot pyramid orchids). In another two minutes skirt round a short stretch of modern wall that extends from the gates of the TA' ZUTA QUARRY No 35 towards the *wied*

The cart-ruts at Ghar il-Kbir. These strange formations occur on many plateau areas on Malta and have puzzled archaeologists, who believe they date from the Bronze Age. In some places, cart-tracks of several different gauges converge.

St Lawrence Chapel (**50min**). From here turn left along a walled-in path; in a further five minutes you reach **Laferla Cross** and the **Annunciation Chapel**. On the summit a spectacular view greets you — a bird's-eye view of the more urban face of Malta.

The track downhill is lined with statues; it meets the SIGGIEWI ROAD at **1h05min**. Turn left on the road and then left again almost immediately. In about five minutes the road swings left at a STONE PILLAR (inscribed GR). Take the track to the right here, passing a FARMHOUSE in a minute. The track deteriorates into a path running between stone walls before improving to a concrete surface. You cross the **Wied il-Luq** on a narrow BRIDGE (**1h15min**) and after 60m/yds cross a road *(Short walk 16-2 comes in from the left here)*. Go straight ahead up a narrow road flanked by small farm buildings. In 15 minutes (**1h30min**) turn left on another road *(where Alternative walk 15-2 comes in from the right)*. After a further 15 minutes of steady climbing, Verdala Palace emerges from the woodland like a French château. Begun in 1586, it was designed as a safe summer retreat for the Grand Master de Verdalle. Once at the boundary wall of **Verdala Palace** (**1h50min**), bear right to the RABAT/BUSKETT ROAD (**1h55min**). The BUS STOP is 50m/yds to the left.

(**30min**). Do not pause at the quarry gates or staff car park; there is much heavy traffic, and workers may be unfriendly towards curious onlookers. (A diversion may be made at this point to a viewpoint over the Girgenti Valley and the Inquisitor's Palace, a summer residence built by Inquisitor Onorati Visconti in the 17th century, by bearing left for 500 metres.)

Follow the road uphill to the right for about two minutes, then go left in front of another QUARRY. A minute later (**33min**), turn right on a narrow country road. *(Short Walk 2 goes left here.)* The road contours round the hill and then turns left to

Map begins on pages 88-89
Distance: 13.5km/8.4mi; 3h20min
Grade: moderate; an ascent of 170m/550ft and descent of 365m/1200ft
Equipment: stout shoes, sunhat, swimwear, waterproofs, picnic, water
How to get there: as Walk 16, page 88
To return: 🚌 201 to Zurrieq (hourly); change to 🚌 71 for Valletta
Short walk: Buskett — Ghar Lapsi (6.4km/4mi; 1h35min; fairly easy). End the walk at Ghar Lapsi to avoid the climb; pre-arrange a taxi pick-up at the Lapsi Restaurant. 🚌 109 runs from Ghar Lapsi to Siggiewi and Rabat (hourly); change to 🚌 62 at Siggiewi for Valletta

Alternative walk: Buskett — Ghar Lapsi — Hagar Qim — Qrendi (11.2km/7.0mi; 2h50min; moderate; an ascent of 180m/600ft and descent of 245m/800ft). Follow the main walk to the Hagar Qim temples, then walk on to the main road. Take the road almost opposite towards Qrendi. On approaching the village, bear right into Misrah Il-Maqluba, to visit the collapsed limestone depression known as Il-Maqluba, adjacent to a chapel dedicated to St Matthew. Follow Triq San Matthew towards the village centre; the 🚌 72 terminus for Valletta is in front of the church.

This walk includes several of Malta's most popular tourist attractions, the prehistoric temples at Hagar Qim and Mnajdra, and the spectacular coastal scenery at the Blue Grotto. It also provides a rare opportunity to visit an under-cliff area.

The walk starts out from the same place as Walk 16, the government's wine and grape research station near the **Buskett Gardens**. Turn right immediately past the WINERY and, after a minute, fork right at the next junction. The single-track road, of indifferent quality, leads to the **Rdum Dikkiena** (Dikkiena Cliffs; **10min**). Turn left here to walk parallel with the coast. At about **18min**, where there is a quarry facility on the left (signed 'RADAM ECO WAYS'), turn right on a stretch of the old road which descends a little towards the sea and follow this until it merges with the main road (**23min**).

At **25min** turn right onto a rocky trail which heads straight for the vertical cliff-edge. Five minutes along, you come to the end of a promontory known as **Il-Wardija ta' San Gorg**. Look carefully for signs of the NEOLITHIC SETTLEMENT here, in-cluding some bell-shaped underground excavations used for the storage of cereals. This area is also home to the national plant, the *Centaurea crassifolia* (Widnet il-Bahar or Malta knap-weed). The track descends in a series of sharp hairpin bends, where the coastal scenery provides a feast for the senses.

At **40min Tal-Karmnu Chapel**, with a fine belvedere, appears. A man-made cave, complete with stone furniture, lies in the small garden below it. Con-tinuing on, the narrow road passes two farmhouses, one of which was owned by Sir Basil Spence, the architect of Coventry Cathedral. **Tal-Lunzjata Chapel** comes up at

about **50min**; there is an information display here about the local area. After passing two converted farmhouses on your left (**1h, 1h05min**), continue straight ahead until the SIGGIEWI/ GHAR LAPSI road is reached (**1h15min**).

Turn right, passing ID-DAR TAL-PROVIDENZA, a home for the disabled, on your right. Reach a roundabout, follow signs for Ghar Lapsi, and in a further two minutes pass a QUARRY on your right. Under two minutes later, a sharp hairpin bend (**1h30min**) signals the start of the descent to Ghar Lapsi. Although there is a water purification plant at **Ghar Lapsi** (**1h45min**; Picnic 17a), there is a lovely cove by the res-taurant, where you can swim and picnic.

So far the walk has been all downhill, but now comes the hard part! Your waymarkers are the two WATER PIPELINES up the cliff. Go back to these water pipes and take a track on the right to the foot of a hill. Cross to the opposite side and proceed uphill on a path. There are rough-hewn steps to assist you at times, but be prepared for some scrambling. It is a steep climb of some 115m/375ft to a building near the top from where a track leads to the HAGAR QIM/ZURRIEQ ROAD (**2h05min**).

Turn right on the road and follow it for about ten minutes. After passing a QUARRY on the right (**2h15min**), turn right on a track by a gate and descend to the floor of an abandoned QUARRY. In a further two minutes, on rounding a corner in the quarry face (on top of which there is a building), *don't*

Left: Verdala Palace and Buskett Gardens (Picnic 16). The high walls once enclosed a deer park.

be tempted to take the path that leads uphill to the left. Instead, continue straight on, passing some old quarry building foundations. A watchtower soon comes into view on the horizon.

From here a rough track takes you downhill to the temples at **Mnajdra** (**2h25min**). The temples are close to the cliff-edge and are protected by a high fence. It is strongly recommended that you approach the temples from the left (landward)

side of the site. From Mnajdra take the paved walkway to the temples of **Hagar Qim** (**2h30min**), where a modern building houses a bar/restaurant and visitor centre.

From here the easiest way to get to the famous Blue Grotto is to turn right on the main ZURRIEQ ROAD, just a minute away. (For those of you with a strong aversion to walking on roads, it is possible (just) to scramble over the pinnacle-like rocks down the *wied* from the

The Blue Grotto — one of Malta's most popular attractions

viewpoint on the road, but the going is very difficult.)

Following the road, you reach the picture-postcard hamlet at the mouth of the **Wied iz-Zurrieq** (Picnic 17b) in **3h05min**. Amongst the colourful boats and boathouses there are boatmen ready to ferry you into the **Blue Grotto** if the sea is calm.

From the hamlet walk back up to the MAIN ROAD (a tiring ascent of 90m/300ft; **3h20min**). Now you have two choices for your return. You can await a bus to Zurrieq, where you change for Valletta. Or, to avoid the change at Zurrieq, you can continue on foot to Qrendi for a mainline bus straight back to Valletta. For the latter, go straight across the main road into a minor road signposted to QRENDI. This leads through pleasant countryside to Misrah Il-Maqluba on the village outskirts. Turn right at a traffic island, where the minor road from Hagar Qim comes in from the left (Alternative walk). Follow TRIQ SAN MATTEW, MISRAH SAN MATTEW and TRIQ IL-PAROCCA to reach the BUS TERMINUS in the *pjazza* in front of the CHURCH (3h40min).

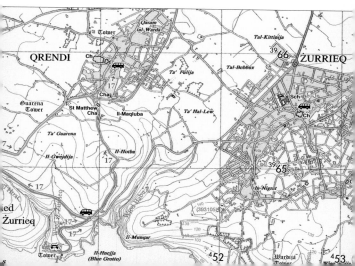

Walk 18 MALTA: SIGGIEWI • TAL-PROVIDENZA • SAN NIKLAW CHAPEL • SIGGIEWI

See map on pages 94-95; see also photograph page 99
Distance: 6.4km/4mi; 1h40min
Grade: very easy, almost level walking
Equipment: stout shoes, sunhat, waterproofs, water
How to get there and return:
🚌 62 from Valletta to Siggiewi (departures every 30min; journey time 40min); alight in the main square.
Short walk: Siggiewi — Tal-Providenza — Siggiewi (3.2km/2mi; 50min; grade as main walk). Follow the main walk for 25min; on reaching Tal-Providenza church, turn left and follow the main walk from the 1h15min-point.

Alternative walk: Siggiewi — Verdala Palace (6.1km/3.8mi; 1h20min; easy, with an ascent of 90m/300ft). Follow the main walk as far as the irrigation tank on the Ghar Lapsi road (14min) and, a minute later, turn right on a narrow asphalt road. Follow this through high stone-walled fields dotted with dozens of small stone storage huts. When you meet the Siggiewi road at a T-junction, turn right. Within two minutes you join the route of Walk 16; use the notes for that walk from the 1h05min-point (page 91) to reach Verdala Palace.

A charming village, richly-farmed countryside, and wayside chapels … everything about this walk conjures up traditional Malta. The bus ride to Siggiewi is fascinating — a windmill, narrow streets lined by old houses with little alleys (known as *sqaq*), and masons crafting ornamental stone in workshops are all to be seen.

Alight at the bus terminus at the lower end of the large L-shaped square (PJAZZA SAN NIKOLA). Pause a moment to soak up the village atmosphere … the church dedicated to St Nicholas (photograph page 99), the clubhouse of the village band, the 'Friend to All' bar, small chapels, political party clubs

Tal-Providenza church

and, in the centre, a statue of the patron saint (St Nicholas) dating from 1734.

Then **start the walk**: turn right past the ST NICHOLAS STATUE, into the lower square. Head for a narrow street flanked by the POLICE STATION and an old CHAPEL (**2min**). Several alleys lead from this street (TRIQ IL-KNISJA L-QADIMA): in ancient times, when pirates and corsairs came ashore to pillage, these could be blocked off easily. At a junction where the streets become much wider (**5min**), continue straight ahead into TRIQ LAPSI (signposted to Ghar Lapsi). The village outskirts and bypass are reached in another three minutes. Follow SIGNS FOR GHAR LAPSI and go straight ahead, into a road. Tal-Providenza church on the horizon provides an un-mistakable landmark, and MARITA FARM HOUSE comes up on your right in **11min**. Two minutes later, at a large irrigation tank, there are fine views back to Siggiewi, while Laferla Cross (Walk 16) and Mdina (Walk 3) can be seen on the right.

At about **25min** leave the road at a GARDEN CENTRE and turn left to **Tal-Providenza** church, with its impressive dome and interesting covered entrance. Turn right along a track, and in two minutes regain the Ghar Lapsi road at two converted farmhouses, TAL-BRIMB and TAL-GHOLJA. No more than two minutes later, at another old WATER TANK which incorporates a MEMORIAL (**30min**), ignore the rather overgrown track on the left. But take the *next* track on the left, 70m/yds further on. This passes a house called LA MIRAGE and twists right and then left, to run parallel with the old QRENDI AIRFIELD (**33min**), where a

runway and hangars were built during World War II to provide additional air support for the Allied invasion of Sicily. Follow its boundary for about 10 minutes, with fine views over intensively-farmed countryside on your left. Towards the end of the airfield (**43min**) the track turns left and, almost imme-diately, right (ignore the cul-de-sac track to the left).

In **50min** you arrive at the small 18th-century **San Niklaw Chapel**. Turn left here, and *beware of dogs* that sometimes guard buildings on both sides of the road. Tal-Providenza is again your goal, and the narrow road descends into a shallow valley dotted with small buildings. At **1h15min** you should be back at a farm complex about 100m/yds east of Tal-Providenza church. Ignore the turn to the right, and in 50m/yds one to the left that would take you back to the church. Instead go straight ahead to regain your outward route, and when you are almost back at the main road turn right at a high walled-in enclosure. Two minutes along, turn left into a very narrow road between high walls. Siggiewi church is now in sight. In about 10 minutes you come to the SIGGIEWI/QRENDI ROAD at a roundabout (**1h28min**). Go straight on, following signs for ZEBBUG and MQABBA. In **1h30min**, at another round-about, ignore the 'Siggiewi Centre' sign; go straight on (towards 'ZEBBUG/QORMI'). In 300m/yds, just before a pedestrian crossing, turn left on TRIQ NIKOLA SAURA. Then follow TRIQ IL-QAJJIED into the main square at **Siggiewi**. The BUS TERMINUS is next to the POLICE STATION (**1h40min**).

Walk 19 MALTA: SIGGIEWI • WIED IL-HESRI • WIED QIRDA • WIED IL-KBIR • QORMI

See also photograph page 22
Distance: 7.2km/4.5mi; 2h05min
Grade: quite easy, some scrambling and rougher walking in the lower Wied Qirda. Do not attempt this walk in wet weather. Descent of 110m/350ft
Equipment: stout shoes, sunhat, waterproofs, water
How to get there: 🚌 62 from Valletta to Siggiewi (departures every 30min; journey time 40min); alight in the main square.
To return: 🚌 62 from Qormi to Valletta
Short walk 1: Siggiewi — Wied il-Hesri — Siggiewi (3.2km/2mi; 50min; easy, with an ascent/descent of 40m/125ft). Follow the main walk and cross the bridge over the Wied il-Hesri. Turn left on a track for about 15 minutes, then leave the valley at the point where a tarmac road leads uphill (near a stone building). This meets a road in a couple of minutes.

Turn left back into the centre of Siggiewi. Return on 🚌 62.
Short walk 2: Siggiewi — Zebbug (2.4km/1.5mi; 40min; easy, with a descent of 50m/175ft). Follow the main walk as far as Hal Mula, on the outskirts of Zebbug, and catch 🚌 62 back to Valletta.

Siggiewi church

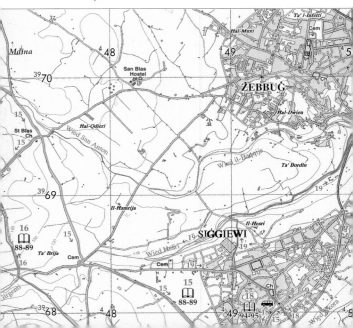

Short walk 3: Zebbug — Qormi
(4.8km/3mi; 1h25min; grade as Short walk 2). Take 🚌 62 as for the main walk, but alight at Hal Mula on the outskirts of Zebbug. Follow the main walk from the 40min-point.

Like Walk 18, this ramble begins at Siggiewi. But this time your route follows a succession of secluded valleys. While some are flanked by cultivated fields, others are so isolated that they have become home to fireworks factories!

Set off from **Siggiewi** by following the one-way signs for traffic leaving the SQUARE, heading northwest along TRIQ IL-PARROCCA. Go through a small square called MISRAH SAN GWANN, then follow TRIQ IL-MITHNA. In just under **5min** you reach a complicated crossroads at the edge of the older part of the village. Turn right along TRIQ WIED IL-HESRI; Mosta Dome should be visible on the horizon. Follow this road to the SIGGIEWI SPORTS COMPLEX (**6min**) and bear right round the sports field, heading downhill. Your way becomes a grassy track through fields, and you descend into the **Wied il-Hesri**. Turn left, cross the BRIDGE and

go right on a narrow tarmac track, parallel with the stream (**13min**). Ignore any tracks on the left which head up the side of the valley (especially the first one: it leads to a fireworks factory; you'll spot warning signs and a red flag). The next landmark is a small TOWER. Not far beyond it, the track crosses the *wied* and, near a group of FARM BUILDINGS, it swings left, away from the *wied* (**25min**). Don't follow the track up to the farm, but bear round to the right, soon returning to the valley floor. At about **35min** the narrow *wied* is sandwiched between an elevated section of the Siggiewi/Zebbug road and high terrace walls.

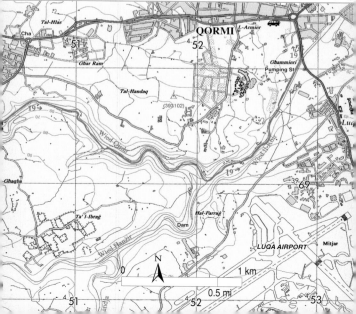

At just under **40min** another *wied* and road come in from the left. A bus stop at **Hal Mula**, on the SIGGIEWI/ZEBBUG ROAD, lies ahead. There is a bus shelter here which may be welcome. Otherwise take the path under the ROAD BRIDGE and continue straight on down the valley, which now becomes the **Wied Qirda**. On your left you can just see an embankment that was intended to carry the main road over the valley; the project was abandoned, and a small public garden was laid out instead (now derelict). The next landfall is the 17th-century chapel shown above, dedicated to the **Visitation of St Elizabeth by Our Lady (45min)**. The building at the rear is a fine example of a fortified farmhouse. Another

farmhouse, opposite, dates from the early 18th century.
Continue past an abandoned farmhouse and another FIREWORKS FACTORY. At **55min** the track swings right. The valley becomes narrower and deeper, and at **1h05min** you pass yet another FIREWORKS FACTORY. Follow a path straight ahead; it gradually descends to the dried-up watercourse in the valley floor. Pick your way along the canyon-like valley, avoiding the large boulders. The path slowly improves to a rough track (**1h40min**), as you leave the narrowest section of the valley.
The **Wied Hanzir** now joins you from the right, and the combined valleys become the **Wied il-Kbir**. An orchard has been planted here. Pass a farmhouse on your left, beyond which the surface of the track improves. Working farms, a garage, greenhouses, a flower nursery, yet another fireworks factory(!) and rooftop guard dogs are your companions now, until you reach the busy QORMI/LUQA ROAD (**2h**). The dome of modern Qormi church is now in sight and the GOVERNMENT FARM is on the opposite side of the road. Turn left and in five minutes reach a roundabout on the outskirts of **Qormi**. Turn left into TRIQ L-IMDINA (a dual carriageway at this point): the BUS STOP for Valletta is only a few yards/metres along to the right.

Walk 20 MALTA: MARSAXLOKK •
WIED HAS-SABTAN • GUDJA

Distance: 8km/5mi; 2h25min
Grade: easy, with an ascent of
130m/425ft and descent of
50m/175ft
Equipment: stout shoes, sunhat,
waterproofs, picnic, water
How to get there: 🚌 81 from

Valletta to Marsaxlokk. Departures
every 20min; journey time about
35-40min
To return: 🚌 135 from Gudja to
University (Tal Qroqq); hourly.
Change to 🚌 31 for Valletta or
Bugibba.

Early societies are a feature of many of the walks in this
book, and in the course of this ramble you can visit a
Bronze Age village and prehistoric cart ruts.

Begin at **Marsaxlokk** by dodging
your way past the quayside
stalls; follow the bay southwards
until the road splits. Ignore the
left fork to Birzebbuga that takes
the easy (but less exciting) way
along the coast to the Ferretti
Battery and Borg in-Nadur.
Instead, follow the road that
climbs slightly to the right (TRIQ
IT-TORRI VERDOME). This leads
into TRIQ IL-KAVALLERIZZA
(**10min**). Head inland on this
street and in 300m/yds pass the
charming **Kavallerizza**, shown
below. Unfortunately, it's now
surrounded by housing
development, but is still visible
at the end of a short street to the
right (**15min**). It was once a
riding school for the Knights.

Just 100m/yds beyond the
house, turn right (signposted
'ZEJTUN'). Rise up for just under
1km/0.6mi, to a three-way
junction (**30min**), where the
main lane bends 90° to the
right. Turn left here on the
higher of two tracks. (A
diversion may be made to the
beautiful Palazzo Il-Marnisi by
bearing right here and
continuing for 400 metres/a
quarter of a mile.)
In a further five minutes, just
after passing an isolated house
on the right with a wooden
balcony (shown below), you
meet a T-junction. The track to
the left is a short-cut, but it
passes two scrapyards with
nasty, unchained dogs. So turn

*You should be able to recognise
the Kavallerizza (opposite),
despite the fact that it's now 'lost'
in a housing estate. Just 20
minutes later, you pass the
isolated house shown below —
recently refurbished and with a
closed wooden balcony. Until a
few years ago, it had wrought-iron
balconies. The traditional Maltese
closed balcony (gallarija) was
always made of wood. Other,
low-maintenance materials have
been used more recently, but they
cannot replicate the traditional
design. Now the Maltese
government offers grants to
promote conservation of the
original wooden structures.*

right here, to the main BIRZEBBUGA ROAD, where there is a BUS STOP. The road is very busy, and there is no pavement. I strongly recommend that you catch a bus and alight at the first stop on the promenade at St George's Bay, a journey of no more than two minutes. On

alighting, cross the road and follow the signs to Borg in-Nadur via TRIQ ALFONSO MARIA GALEA, go right into SQAQ IN-NADUR, and take the path up to the defensive wall, which in some places is as high as 5m/15ft. Excavation work carried out here in the 1930s

Harbour at Marsaxlokk

BIRZEBBUGA) and, after a few yards/metres, turn right on TRIQ ID-DAR TA' PULTU. This narrow lane soon becomes a farm track between terraced fields, and in just under five minutes ends at a WIRE MESH GATE. Fork right here, on a path leading out to a stone surface above the **Wied Has-Sabtan**. In another six or seven minutes, when you come to a small stone hut, the path swings to the right, crosses over two pipes and turns left at a higher level.

About **1h40min** should see you at a dilapidated farm, the CASA IPPOLITA, which was built in 1664 by a Sicilian nobleman. Turn left and descend towards the valley floor, re-crossing the twin pipes on your way. Your next target is a SMALL, GREY-COLOURED BUILDING with an awning in a secluded position near the valley floor. In a few minutes the path, now a grassy track, crosses the head of the **Wied il-Qoton** (a tributary of the Wied Has Sabtan), which is narrow and shallow at this point. When you encounter a track (**1h50min**), turn right to cross both *wieds*. By now the track has improved to a poorly-surfaced road. A magnificent PILLBOX incorporated into a house and PILLAR are landmarks in the next ten minutes. Take a rough track on your left between high dry-stone walls. At a crossroads of sorts (**2h05min**), continue straight ahead on a very narrow road.

On the outskirts of **Gudja**, take TRIQ SAN GORG and TRIQ SAN CIRU to the CHURCH. Turn right here and, almost immediately, go left on TRIQ WILLIAM BAKER. In 250m/yds you reach a public garden and BUS STOP (**2h25min**).

revealed a Bronze Age village site and fortifications, a Copper Age temple site and prehistoric cart-ruts.

Retrace your steps to the water-front and take the road towards Birzebbuga. At the junction two to three minutes later, take the fork furthest to the right (TRIQ

Walk 21 MALTA: MARSASCALA • ST THOMAS BAY • FORT DELIMARA • MARSAXLOKK

See also photographs on pages 102-103, 107 and 109

Distance: 9.9km/6.2mi; 2h30min

Grade: fairly easy, with overall ascent/descent of 110m/350ft

Equipment: stout shoes, sunhat, swimwear, waterproofs, picnic, water

How to get there: 🚌 91 from Valletta to Marsascala (departures every 10min; journey time 35min) or 🚌 124 from Vittoriosa/Cospicua via Zabbar to Marsascala (departures hourly; journey time 25-30min). Alight in the village centre where there are bars and cafes, or stay on the bus until it reaches St Thomas Bay, a saving of 35min.

To return: 🚌 81 from Marsaxlokk to Valletta

View north from Tal-Munxar towards St Thomas Bay and Marsascala

This walk introduces 'Landscapers' to two contrasting communities on the southeast coast. Marsascala has become a fashionable place to live and has a number of cafés and restaurants on its promenade — ideal for a coffee or snack before starting Walk 21 or 22. Marsaxlokk is still a working port, and the brightly coloured boats and quayside market are popular with visitors. Unfortunately the deep waters of Marsaxlokk Bay have also attracted a container terminal and a power station.

Start out in **Marsascala** by walking around Marsascala Bay to the redoubt shown on page 109, the **St Thomas Tower**. Just beyond the (closed) JERMA PALACE HOTEL, you have two options. *In good weather,* cut down to the SALT PANS on the beach and scramble along the rocky foreshore. On coming to a PILLBOX (**25min**), climb up to the low cliff jutting into St Thomas Bay, where you will arrive at a PUBLIC GARDEN (Picnic 21a; **35min**). *In wet weather,* it's best to take roads to the garden: begin by following TRIQ IR-RIDOTT which becomes TRIQ THOMAS ASHBY, turn right into TRIQ PHILIPPE DE VENDOME, and then go left on a wide road (TRIQ IL-QALIET). This takes you to the PUBLIC GARDEN in **35min**.

Walk to the far end of the garden, where a restaurant overlooks **St Thomas Bay**. Carry on along the shore, passing holiday homes, to the far end. At a farm building, take the right-hand fork, going uphill on a rough track between stone walls; you pass the small **St Paul Chapel** (**55min**).

Some 200m/yds beyond the chapel, join a narrow road that

Low cliffs on the outskirts of Marsascala

comes in from the **Xrobb il-Ghagin Peninsula**. In five minutes (**1h05min**), after passing some bushes, go left on a track (at a single leaning tree, where the narrow road turns sharply to the right). After 30m/yds this track swings to the right. Follow it for just two minutes, to a small FARM BUILDING. Descend a few yards/metres as you pass this building. An entrance to a field on your left is blocked by a wooden gate; your way is straight ahead on a terraced shelf between a field wall on your right and a cultivated terrace some 6 feet/2m below. Continue along the edge of terraced fields until you meet a track coming from the right (**1h12min**).

Coastal erosion affecting the cliffs beyond this point means that for safety reasons an inland route is followed. Take the track and, in two minutes, reach a minor road running from Marsaxlokk to Delimara Point. Turn left here to visit **Fort Delimara** (**1h30min**). The fort, built by the British in 1881, is an impressive stronghold with a deep ditch, but is not open to the public. There are fine views from the entrance towards the container port at Kalafrana.

From the fort entrance, retrace your steps and follow the ridge road, passing the POWER STATION and, on the opposite side of the road, L-GHARIX, the residence of Dom Mintoff, a former Prime Minister of Malta (**1h50min**). Keep to this quiet road as far as **Tas-Silg Battery** (**2h15min**) and, from there, take a track on the left down to the ACCESS ROAD for the power station. Turn right and in 50m/yds turn left on a road to colourful **Marsaxlokk** (**2h30min**), Malta's largest fishing village. Visit the open-air market, before boarding your bus in the main street.

Market and harbour at Marsaxxlokk

Walk 22 MALTA: MARSASCALA • ZONQOR POINT • XGHAJRA • MARSASCALA

Distance: 9.1km/5.7mi; 2h10min
Grade: easy, with an ascent of 220m/350ft and descent of 90m/300ft
Equipment: stout shoes, sunhat, waterproofs, water, picnic
How to get there and return:
🚌 91 from Valletta to Marsascala (departures every 10min; journey time 35min) or 🚌 124 from Vittoriosa/Cospicua via Zabbar to Marsascala (departures hourly; journey time 25-30min). Alight at Marsascala church. Return using the same bus services, as described on page 110.

Short walk 1: Marsascala — Zonqor Point — Blata l–Bajda — Xghajra (5km/3.1mi; 1h30min; easy, with an ascent/descent of 50m/175ft). Follow the main walk as far as the pillbox (50min), cut down to the coastal path, and turn left to Xghajra's church. Return from there on 🚌 3 to Valletta.
Short walk 2: Xghajra — Blata l–Bajda — Marsascala (3.5km/2.2mi; 1h05min; easy, with an ascent of 45m/150ft and descent of 30m/100ft). Take 🚌 3 from Valletta to the bus stop at Xghajra church on Triq il-Knisja. Follow the main walk from there to Marsascala.

This is a walk of contrasts: the ridge provides easy walking, with fine views and some architectural curiosities, while the coastal stretch closely hugs the sea, weaving its way among coves and promontories, from watchtowers to forts.

Begin the walk at Marsascala church: head off around the north side of the pretty bay. It is possible to pass in front of the houses at the water's edge during the first part of the walk. **Zonqor Point (18min)** is your next landmark, with views across the bay to St Thomas Tower. From here retrace your steps for about three minutes, then turn right uphill on TRIQ IL-BLAJJIET. Turn right again along TRIQ GHAXQET I-GHAJN (**30min**).

The walk begins at Marsascala's church, with its prominent tower (backed by building works when the route was rechecked).

Follow this around until it rejoins TRIQ IL-BLAJJIET, where you turn right downhill. After 100m/yds take a narrow, roughly surfaced road on the right (**40min**). This passes a farm, then swings round to the left and becomes wider. The going is easy from now on, affording pleasant walking and good views of the valley to the west. You pass by the lovely little CHAPEL shown overleaf (**45min**; it dates from 1761). A large World War II PILLBOX is your next landmark less than five minutes later (**47min**). *(Short walk 1 cuts down to the coastal path here.)* Soon **Fort San Leonardo** is visible on your right, dating from the late 19th century but now much neglected and used for agricultural purposes.

After passing several large farms (**57min**), the road swings round to the right. On the next bend,

you come to the ruins of an old house incorporating a chapel. Another ten minutes brings you to the TAL-MILORD CONCRETE MIX works, on your left close to a farm. Just before reaching the roundabout on the outskirts of Xghajra (just over **1h10min**), a short stretch of old country lane (SQAQ SAN LEONARDO) can be seen beside a farmhouse. Turn right at the roundabout, and in a few minutes bear left on TRIQ ORLANDO ZABBAR (with a 'no entry' sign). This pedestrianised street leads into TRIQ IL-KNISJA and the centre of **Xghajra**, a resort frequented by the Maltese. Make for the coast with its skyline of many watchtowers, and turn back southeast towards Marsascala on a promenade. Just past Xghajra, the San Leonardo Fort, high on the horizon on the right, overlooks the walk. Continue along the promenade to the salt pans at

This 18th-century chapel is passed 45min into the walk.

Blata l-Bajda — the next landmark (Picnic 22).

The little bay of **Gorf l-Abjad** (The White Gulf) comes up at the **1h45min**-mark, by which time your route has become a path. Ten minutes later, by a small inlet where there are two PILLBOXES and a WATCHTOWER, climb up right, to a track. Follow the track steeply uphill for five minutes, to regain the ridge road (**2h**) by the large PILLBOX encountered on the outward journey.

Walk straight ahead downhill on a narrow road through terraced fields. In under ten minutes you reach the MARSASCALA-ZABBAR ROAD (**2h10min**), where you should catch the bus in either the direction of Marsascala or Valletta and Cospicua.

St Thomas Tower (visited on Walk 21)

Walk 23 GOZO: VICTORIA • ZEBBUG • XWIENI BAY • HEKKA POINT • GHARB • VICTORIA

Distance: 16km/10mi; 4h10min
Grade: easy with some rougher walking towards Hekka Point; overall ascent/descent 170m/550ft
Equipment: stout shoes, sunhat, waterproofs, water, picnic
How to get there and return: 🚢 from Malta to Mgarr Harbour, then 🚌 301 from Mgarr to Victoria; journey time 15min
Short walk: Ghasri — Wied il-Ghasri — Gordan Lighthouse — Ghasri (4.2km/2.6mi; 55min; easy, with an ascent/descent of 115m/370ft. From the square in Ghasri (Pjazza Salvatur) fork left along Triq Salvu Gambin and in one minute turn left into Triq il-Knisja. In about 10 minutes pass a stone cross and Tal-Patrocinju church, the oldest on Gozo. Turn left along Triq il-Gonna. In about three minutes, where a road (Triq il-Fanal) comes in from the left, turn right and follow this to Gordan Lighthouse (30min). The return route is straight along Triq il-Fanal to the Ghammar/Ghasri road, where you turn left.
Shorter walk 1: Victoria — Ghasri — Victoria (11.2km/7mi; 3h; easy, with an ascent/descent of 30m/100ft). Follow the main walk to the Wied il-Ghasri, but then turn left up the rough track, to the village of Ghasri, from where you can return to Victoria by road.
Shorter walk 2: Victoria — Zebbug — Wied il-Ghasri — Xwieni Bay — Marsalforn (8.5km/5.3mi; 2h55min; easy ascent of 30m/100ft and descent of 140m/450ft). Follow the main walk to Zebbug. Bear left at the church, along Triq il-Knisja and Triq il-Madonna ta' Cicri, then turn left on Triq Caqra (Picnic 23a is three minutes straight on, via Triq Onice). Continue downhill on a track for 10 minutes, then go straight ahead at a crossroads (by a converted farmhouse). One minute later, when the track swings round to the right, follow it towards the coast and rejoin the main walk at the 2h05min-point. Now use the map to walk to Xwieni Bay and Marsalforn (the main walk in reverse). Return to Victoria on 🚌 306 or to Mgarr on 🚌 322.
Alternative walk: Victoria — Zebbug — Wied il-Ghasri — Hekka Point — Birbuba — Santu Pietru — San Lawrenz — Dwejra Bay (14.2km/8.9mi; 3h55min; grade as main walk, with a descent of 260m/850ft). Follow Shorter walk 2 to the point where it rejoins the main walk. Follow the main walk from the 2h05min-point to Birbuba (3h10min). Five minutes later, instead of going straight on towards Gharb, turn right into Triq Mongur. On coming into Santu Pietru, turn right in the square, then go left three minutes later, along Triq il-Wileg. When you reach the church at San Lawrenz, turn right along Triq id-Duluri and follow the road to Dwejra Bay (Walk 24; see map pages 116-117). Return on 🚌 302 to Victoria, or use the notes on page 118 to walk to Victoria.

A pleasant stroll through a patchwork of fields links Victoria with the large hilltop village of Zebbug. A steep descent then takes us to the coastal salt pans. Then we cross a long stretch of coastal terrain, before returning to village life at Gharb.

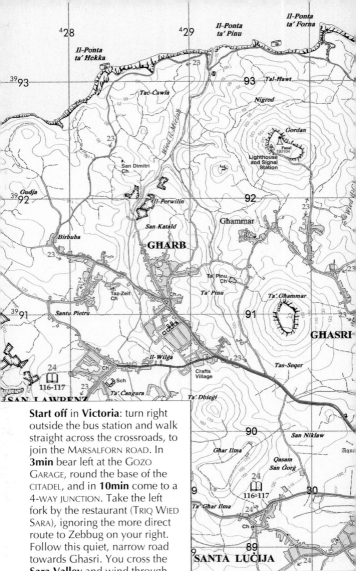

Start off in **Victoria**: turn right outside the bus station and walk straight across the crossroads, to join the MARSALFORN ROAD. In **3min** bear left at the GOZO GARAGE, round the base of the CITADEL, and in **10min** come to a 4-WAY JUNCTION. Take the left fork by the restaurant (TRIQ WIED SARA), ignoring the more direct route to Zebbug on your right. Follow this quiet, narrow road towards Ghasri. You cross the **Sara Valley** and wind through tiny green fields interrupted by tabletop hills. Ghasri church comes into view after ten minutes (**20min**). Five minutes later, on reaching the outskirts of **Ghasri**, turn right (**25min**). You pass a small CEMETERY four minutes later and come to a much larger CEMETERY at about the **35min**-mark. Bear left here,

112

shortly afterwards beginning the climb to **Zebbug**, a delightful hilltop village. Take the street to the right of the church and follow it to the far end of the village, from where the road descends to the coast via hairpin bends. Spectacular views over the salt pans and the strange coastal rock formations, remi-

niscent of Neapolitan ice cream, accompany you on this steep descent.

Xwieni Bay (Picnic 23b) is reached at about **1h30min**; its name derives from the galley-shaped rock that dominates it. Turn left around the bay, along an undulating concrete road that acquires a tarmac surface after 15 minutes. At about **1h55min** turn right on another narrow tarmac road which leads into a shallow little valley. The road soon peters out into a rough track. Where it ends, bear left and follow a path parallel with the **Wied il-Ghasri** for a few minutes. The path gradually improves to a track.

113

Observe a farm on the opposite side of the *wied*; some 150m/yds after passing the farm, the *wied* becomes shallow (**2h05min**). *(Shorter walk 1 turns left here; Shorter walk 2 and the Alternative walk rejoin the main walk here).* Cross over to the other side and turn right, passing the afore-mentioned farm. Ignore the narrow track on the left immediately after the farm; soon your track runs parallel with the cliffs (**2h10min**). Gordan lighthouse stands on the hill to your left. When you reach the **Wied il-Mielah** (**2h25min**), another road comes in (from Gharb.) At the entrance to this *wied* there is a spectacular arch in the sea cliffs (add five minutes if you detour to the cliffs, and keep a safe distance from the edge).

Top: Xwieni Bay and saltpans; above: Forna Point

Cross the bridge over the Wied il-Mielah and take the concrete road on the west side of the valley. This soon becomes a rough track and leads into an area where the wind has eroded the softer limestone (**2h33min**). Continue to an eroded area that resembles a quarry (**2h37min**). Almost immediately past the depression, take a rough path up to the higher cliff shelf on your left. The path is quite wide just before the higher level is reached. Once on the higher ground (**2h40min**), turn right and carry on over rough terrain. A track at the western end, some 500m/yds distant, becomes your target, and this overlooks wild and barren **Hekka Point** (**2h50min**).

Follow the track inland and turn left at the ruins of a FIREWORKS FACTORY (**2h55min**). Two minutes later, bear right at TWO SMALL STONE BUILDINGS (one has the word 'Barra' painted on it) and proceed along a narrow road that becomes TRIQ TA' SAN DIMITRI (San Dimitri Church is a short distance away to the left). The road meanders into the picturesque hamlet of **Birbuba** (**3h10min**). *(The Alternative walk turns right in a further five minutes).*

When you arrive at **Gharb** (**3h25min**), pause for a moment in the main square by the police station, to admire the traditional architecture and fine market cross. There is a folk museum in the square and the local council have been actively signposting nearby places of interest. It is possible to catch a bus from Gharb back to Victoria. For those who prefer to walk, the main SAN LAWRENZ/VICTORIA ROAD is reached about ten minutes. Turn left and, after passing the hill known as **Gelmus Butte** on your left, you should arrive in **Victoria** after about **4h10min**.

Walk 24 GOZO: VICTORIA • XLENDI • DWEJRA BAY • SANTA LUCIJA • VICTORIA

See also photograph page 25
Distance: 16.3km/10.2mi; 5h
Grade: easy, except for the steep ascent out of Xlendi, which is only recommended for robust walkers (Alternative walk 2 avoids this ascent). Overall ascent/descent of 270m/875ft
Equipment: stout shoes, sunhat, swimwear, waterproofs, picnic, water
How to get there and return: as Walk 23, page 111
Short walk: Victoria — Xlendi — Victoria (7.3km/4.5mi; 1h40min; easy, with an ascent/descent of 90m/350ft). Follow the main walk to Xlendi, then take the road up the Xlendi Valley directly back to Victoria.
Alternative walk 1: Victoria — Kercem — Dwejra Bay — Victoria (13.6km/8.5mi; 3h50min; easy, with an ascent/descent of 160m/525ft). Take the road from Victoria to Kercem and join the main walk along the ridge road which runs parallel with Xlendi Bay. Pick up the notes for the main walk at the 1h45min-point.

Alternative walk 2: Victoria — Xlendi — Kercem — Dwejra Bay — Santa Lucija — Victoria (20.2km/12.6mi; 5h; easy; ascent 160m/525ft, descent 270m/875ft). This route avoids the steep rocky ascent from Xlendi. Follow the main walk to Xlendi, then walk up the road towards Victoria. 15min from Xlendi, at a tiny crossroads by a bus shelter, turn left on a narrow road winding uphill through fields towards the ridge. You reach the hamlet of Ta' Ghajn Tuta in 5min. Here turn left towards the sea on a narrow road. Ignore all tracks left and right; continue above the fields. 35min from Xlendi, on the outskirts of Kercem, take the first road on the left (opposite a house, Mater Dolorosa). In 2min turn left by a bus stop. In another 2min, at a post box, go left along Triq Qasam San Pawl. Ignore a road on the left in 5min and one on the right a minute later. A few minutes later a track comes in from the left: you have rejoined the main walk at the 1h45min-point; follow it to its end.

Cliffs at Dwejra Bay

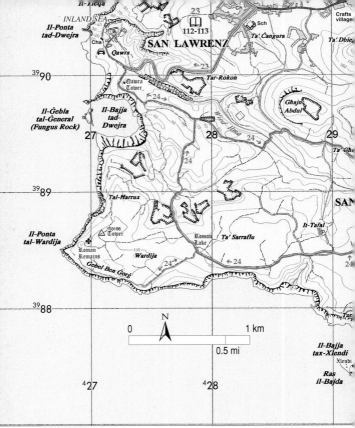

T his walk visits the fishing village of Xlendi — probably Gozo's favourite attraction, as well as Fungus Rock, the Dwejra Arch and the Inland Sea — the island's most spectacular coastal rock formations.

Start out at the BUS STATION in **Victoria**: turn left and follow SIGNPOSTING TO XLENDI. In **5min** continue straight on for Munxar (where the road forks right to Xlendi). Turn right into the outskirts of **Munxar** at **20min** and pass the CHURCH and square. Fork left on TRIQ DUN SPIR GAUCI and climb in a southerly direction. In two minutes (**22min**) turn right and then immediately left, into TRIQ ZGHAWRI (also signposted to the Sanap Cliffs).

Strike off right again in **30min**, ignoring a road on your left

which leads to the Sanap Cliffs (the detour to the viewpoint takes about six minutes return). Follow the road parallel with the coast (but some distance inland). In **40min**, at the second of two turn-offs that follow each other in rapid succession, turn left on a track which soon turns into a path. It runs into the river bed, which is flanked by stone walls, and then heads straight for the cliffs. Just before a ruined building, bear left again and, at **50min**, turn right over a STONE FOOTBRIDGE at the head of a fjord-like inlet. (The curious

may now divert to Xlendi Tower on the point.) The sandy bay at **Xlendi** (**1h**), sheltering between sheer cliffs, must be one of the most visited spots on the island (Picnic 24a).

Carry on to the far side of the bay, noting the position of the STONE CRAB RESTAURANT: just beyond it there is a steep climb up the steps cut into the cliff-face. Turn right at the top of the steps and follow a cliff path to a position level with the back of the afore-mentioned restaurant. Look in the cliff-face for steps cut into the rock and head uphill to a plateau. Try to maintain a climbing angle of 45° until you reach a point almost opposite an open-air bar on the far side of the bay. At this point, a path leads more directly uphill, towards the remains of a stone wall. Continue walking for about one minute, *taking care to keep a safe distance from the cliffs which encroach at this point,* and follow a path inland. On joining a track, follow it around to the right; then, a minute later, turn left on a concrete-surfaced track that turns inland for about 10 minutes until it meets a minor road (**1h45min**) running along the TOP OF THE RIDGE. Follow this to the left (westwards). Ignore the right turn about three minutes along. At a fork, keep left and follow the white arrow. Two red and white masts stand some 250m/yds away on your right.

Approaching Xlendi Bay

At around **2h** you come to a little pond in the rock (the ROMAN LAKE). Here a diversion may be made to Wardija Point, an important ancient site: the turn-off is opposite the pond.

The main walk bears right immediately after passing the pond. Five minutes later, at a downhill bend soon after passing between two quarries, turn right. Then, almost immediately, turn left (the fork to the right would take you into a quarry). One minute later, go left again at a cane windbreak, taking a track down into a shallow *wied.*

After crossing the *wied* the track climbs up through terraces. At one point the track has become blocked by stones that have fallen from the adjacent embankment. It is necessary to divert left onto a path in the adjacent field which has been kept free of cultivation. Beyond the obstruction, the path meets a footpath, where you head left to **Qawra Tower (2h45min)**.

Below is **Dwejra Bay**, which was once completely encircled by land. **Fungus Rock** (photograph page 26) is now all that remains of its outer rim. The rock was notable as the habitat

of a rare fungus highly prized by the Knights for its medicinal properties.

From the tower make your way around to the rock arch and tiny CHAPEL at **Dwejra** and thence to the **Inland Sea** between the chapel and the cliffs (**3h15min**). This magnificent area, shown on page 115, takes on an almost mystical character when drenched in a fine sea-spray mist. The Inland Sea is an enormous collapsed cave, still with a tunnel to the open sea. Local fishermen provide boat trips through the tunnel to view the high, almost vertical cliffs on the ther side. To really appreciate the area, climb up past the chapel and walk round the rim of the crater.

Now retrace your steps back past Qawra Tower. At the point where the footpath meets the track you climbed from the *wied* (**4h**), continue straight ahead on a narrow path, passing a QUARRY BUILDING. Ten minutes later, turn left at a track crossroads (beside a large house). A narrow BRIDGE takes you across the **Wied Ilma** and, in a few minutes, you bear right at a farmhouse, where a welcome SPRING feeds water into roadside troughs. On the hillside above are ancient caves which housed some of Gozo's earliest inhabitants.

A small road leads you into the pretty village of **Santa Lucija** at just under **4h30min**. Head out by bearing left at the peaceful square and then go along a road thinly lined with trees. Once past the pumping station and RESERVOIR, you will be well on your way back to **Victoria** (**5h**).

Walk 25 GOZO: MGARR • MGARR IX-XINI • SANNAT • VICTORIA

See also photograph page 25
Distance: 7.5km/4.7mi; 2h45min
Grade: moderate; some scrambling between Mgarr and Mgarr ix-Xini. Ascent about 180m/600ft, descent 75m/250ft
Equipment: stout shoes, sunhat, swimwear, waterproofs, picnic, water
How to get there and return:
🚢 between Malta and Mgarr Harbour; if staying in Gozo, 🚌 301, 302 from Victoria to Mgarr; journey time 15min.
Short walk: Mgarr — Mgarr ix-Xini — Mgarr (4.3km/2.7mi to the tower; 1h15min; moderate, with an ascent of 140m/450ft and descent of 40m/125ft). Follow the main walk to Mgarr ix-Xini but, instead of crossing the bay, keep to its eastern side

and follow the rough road up to the former heliport and Santa Cilja Tower. Catch 🚌 301 to Victoria or Mgarr Harbour, or walk along the main road to the harbour. (It is also possible to use a parallel minor road on the right, just before the (disused) heliport; this leads into Triq Ta' Cordina in Ghajnsielem).
Alternative walk: Mgarr — Xewkija (6.7km/4.2mi; 2h; grade as Short walk 1). Follow the main walk to Mgarr ix-Xini. Cross to the western side of the bay and take the narrow road up the Wied Hanzira. Turn right through Xewkija and follow the map to the traffic lights on the north side of the village, where you can catch 🚌 301 to Victoria or Mgarr.

T he hustle and bustle of the ferry port of Mgarr are soon left behind as the walk heads westwards towards the highest cliffs in Gozo. The final stretch takes in the sprawling village of Sannat and the southern suburbs of Victoria.

Start the walk at **Mgarr harbour**: leave the harbour area and walk uphill on SHORT STREET. In **5min** turn left at VELSON'S WINERY into TRIQ LOURDES. In a few minutes, near the top of the hill, rejoin the main MGARR/VICTORIA ROAD near Fort Chambray, which has impressive walls and ditches. The fort dates from 1749 and was one of the last major projects during the rule of the Knights of St John. Today a housing development is in progress. Proceed along the main road and in just under five minutes (**15min**) turn left along TRIQ TA' CORDINA (there is a house called THE HAVEN at the junction). Your route follows

some sleepy streets on the outskirts of the village of **Ghajnsielem**. First, in a few yards/metres bear right at FRANK'S GARAGE; then, a minute later, take a left turn onto a concrete track (TRIQ IX-XATT L-AHMAR) that leads downhill. Pass a small POND fringed by bamboo. Continue downhill; the track becomes a path running parallel with the course of a stream flanked by bamboo. Follow this to a group of BOAT HOUSES (**25min**).
Continue along the coastal track, passing saltpans and a splendid PRICKLY PEAR HEDGE (**30min**). Just past the hedge a minor road comes down from Ghajnsielem; there is parking

119

and seats here, as well as a local INFORMATION BOARD. For those interested in military weaponry, there is a FOUGASSE on the foreshore that was used to discourage pirates. Your way becomes a footpath which runs parallel with the fields, on their seaward side. In just over **45min** you descend to a ROCK-CUT PLAT-FORM, where there are more SALTPANS (and a sewage outfall). After a prolonged spell of wet weather, it is likely that you will encounter a stream flowing over part of the rock-cut platform; *care* and some scrambling will be needed to get round this obstacle.

You will see your next land-mark, the tower guarding the entrance to **Mgarr ix-Xini** inlet; it is reached in under **1h**. This steep-sided valley was probably the main port used by the Knights of Malta (the name means Harbour for Galleys) and is a lovely swimming, boating and fishing spot (Picnic 25).

It will take you almost 15 minutes to reach the crossing point of the *wied*. Once on the other side, take the small road to the right, pass the WATER TANK and, 50m/yds further on, at a passing place on the road, turn left through a gap in the wall.

Join a road that after three minutes acquires a tarmac surface and follow it south, winding through holiday bungalows. Fine views of the bay and tower should inspire you. At the bungalow TINA (**1h25min**), turn left on a track and, a few minutes later, turn left again. **Wied Sabbar** is crossed by a BRIDGE. The going is all uphill now, until the majestic cliff-tops are reached. In another five minutes bear left, following the cliffs (ignoring the right fork which runs parallel with the *wied*). Two to three minutes later, just before reaching a headland, take a path on the

right, which rises to a track in two minutes.

Turn left on an increasingly ill-defined track which initially runs parallel with the cliffs but after two minutes turns uphill to the head of the *wied* in a further three-four minutes (**1h40min**). Ignoring the right fork across a bridge, continue straight ahead. A lone tree and the low outline of a hotel in the distance are your landmarks. This track crosses an area of great archaeological interest and provides panoramic views of the splendid vertical cliffs on both Malta and Gozo. On your right, a few minutes from the track, lie the

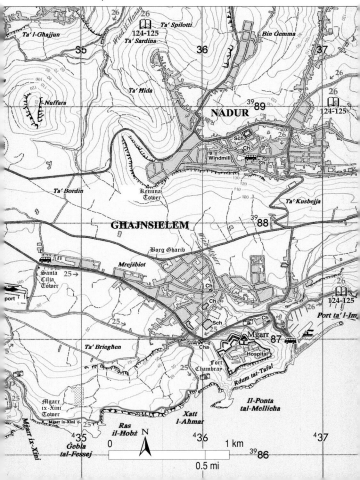

Above: Mgarr ix-Xini; left Xewkija church seen from near Ta' Cenc (top) and (below): cliffs at Ta' Cenc

remains of **Il Borg Ta' L-Imramma**, a Copper Age temple. A few minutes later, cart ruts of two different gauges can be found by taking a diversion just before reaching the boundary of the HOTEL TA' CENC (**2h**). Turn left on a good track towards the cliffs and in four minutes, where it bears away to the left, continue straight ahead on a red-earth path until, after five minutes, the low wall on your right ends. Turn right and in 100m/yds come to short section of wall near the edge of the high vertical cliffs. Good examples of cart ruts can be found on the landward side of the wall. This diversion *adds 15min* to the overall times. *Great care is needed when approaching the cliffs in this area.*

Bear right around the hotel and ten minutes later you will be in the centre of the pristine village of **Sannat**. You could catch a bus to Victoria here; otherwise walk on to **Victoria** by road (**2h45min**).

Walk 26 GOZO: MGARR • HONDOQ IR-RUMMIEN • QALA • DAHLET QORROT • SAN BLAS BAY • IR-RAMLA • XAGHRA

See also photos pages 14, 25, 33
Distance: 14.6km/9mi; 4h05min
Grade: moderate to difficult; overall ascent of about 520m/ 1700ft and descent of 460m/ 1500ft (depending on the route). Possibility of vertigo on the coastal path to Hondoq ir-Rummien: *in wet weather use the Short walk route.* Some rough terrain near Dahlet Qorrot. Beyond Dahlet Qorrot the walking is moderate, but sometimes steep.
Equipment: walking boots or stout shoes, sunhat, swimwear, waterproofs, picnic, water
How to get there: as Walk 24, page 119
To return: 🚐 322 to Mgarr (via Marsalforn) or change at Marsalforn to 🚐 306 for Victoria and Xlendi

Short walk: Mgarr — Hondoq ir-Rummien — Qala — Mgarr (4km/2.5mi; 1h40min; moderate, with ascent/descent of 180m/600ft). Follow the main walk to the defensive wall (25min). Some 20m/yds from

the eastern end of the wall, take a path which leads to a track with a prickly pear hedge on the left and a wall on the right. After passing an abandoned building, bear right. Concrete comes under foot, and you meet a road coming down from Qala. Turn left here, to rise 60m/200ft to Qala. Turn left on Triq iz-Zew-wieqa (fine views to Comino and Mgarr harbour). Follow this road downhill, turning left in Mgarr to the harbour.

Alternative walk: Mgarr — Hondoq ir-Rummien — Qala — Nadur (7.5km/4.7mi; 2h; moderate, with an ascent of 230m/750ft and descent of 205m/675ft). Follow the main walk to the 1h20min-point. Instead of turning right towards the coast, bear left and then right, to reach the Nadur/Dahlet Qorrot road. Head left into the centre of Nadur; the stop for 🚐 303 to Victoria or 303, 322 to Mgarr is in the square next to the church.

This is the most arduous walk in the Gozo series. Like Walk 23, it takes in an area not visited by many tourists. On offer are rugged cliffs, two lovely coves and the best beach on the island.

The walk starts in **Mgarr**, at the GLENEAGLES BAR on the water-front, where colourful fishing boats lie at anchor. Follow the road around the north side of the harbour, passing the MARINA and the SEAPLANE TERMINAL. The road ends at a BREAKWATER (**10min**). Scramble through some rocks on the foreshore for a short distance, and then take the footpath leading to a DEFENSIVE WALL (**25min**) guarding a route inland. About 20m/yds before the

eastern end of the defensive wall, take the path to the top of the wall *(the Short walk starts here)* and follow the coast, keeping to the highest path (ie, the furthest inland), away from the cliff-edge. There is a risk of vertigo here. *(In wet weather you should follow the Short walk above, then turn right at the road from Qala. When it ends at a deserted farmhouse, go left round the building and follow a path back to the coast. Add 5-7 minutes to all timings.)*

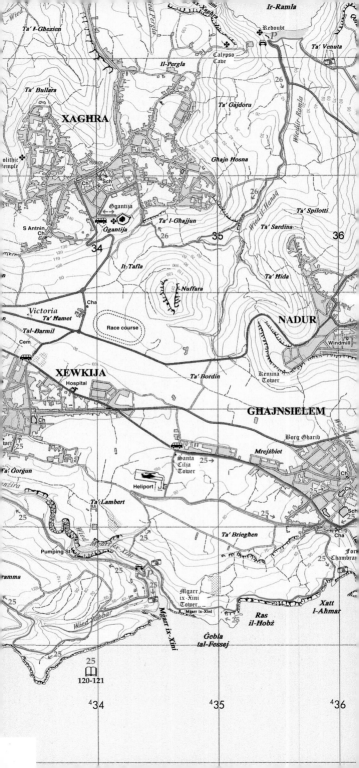

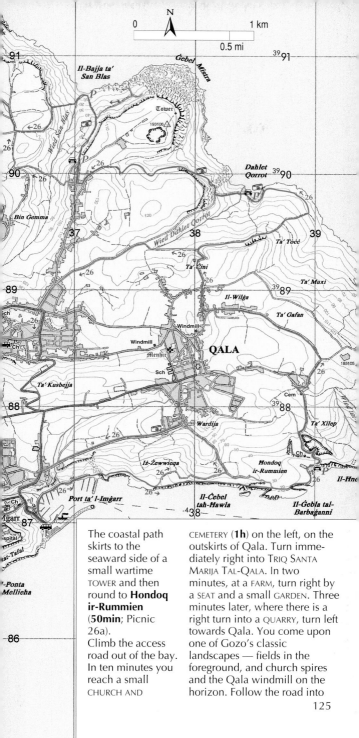

The coastal path skirts to the seaward side of a small wartime TOWER and then round to **Hondoq ir-Rummien** (**50min**; Picnic 26a).
Climb the access road out of the bay. In ten minutes you reach a small CHURCH AND CEMETERY (**1h**) on the left, on the outskirts of Qala. Turn immediately right into TRIQ SANTA MARIJA TAL-QALA. In two minutes, at a FARM, turn right by a SEAT and a small GARDEN. Three minutes later, where there is a right turn into a QUARRY, turn left towards Qala. You come upon one of Gozo's classic landscapes — fields in the foreground, and church spires and the Qala windmill on the horizon. Follow the road into

Qala. Bear right into a narrow street (TRIQ TA'SEMPER; **1h12min**). Then turn right into TRIQ IL-MITHNA; a house at this junction is dated USA 1983 and has sunflower decorations on its balconies. (A short detour to the left would take you to the privately-owned windmill.) At a crossroads reached in little more than one minute, continue straight ahead into TRIQ TA'GULJU. Four minutes later the track descends steeply. Soon you meet a fork: go right (the Alternative walk goes left here). Descend gradually to a small WATCHTOWER (**1h35min**). Continue towards the coast and turn left on the coastal path. After ten minutes some steps take you down to **Dahlet Qorrot** (**1h50min**; Picnic 26b). This colourful bay, with its boat houses built into the cliff, provides a good cooling-off point in the summer.

Carry on around the bay, taking the minor road up the western side. At **1h55min**, 50m/yds past some prickly pears, follow a track to the right, just below the cliff, and make your way around the hill. After about ten minutes (**2h05min**), come to a TANK at the foot of the cliff and cross over a PIPE, bearing left uphill. The footpath leads into a track, passing a CITRUS FARM, and emerges on a ROAD (**2h15min**). Turn left and, on the outskirts of **Nadur**, take the first right (opposite a FARMHOUSE WITH A PLAQUE AND SHRINE on its front

wall).* Then bear right again at VILLA SAN BLAS. Just after passing a small garden (**2h20min**; Picnic 26c) the road takes you down into **San Blas Bay** (**2h30min**; Picnic 26d). Just before the bottom of the road, take the left-hand fork, passing cane windbreaks sheltering citrus groves.**

From the beach (very popular with the local people) proceed initially up the watercourse of the **San Blas Valley**, passing the fishermen's huts. Then cross the stream and bear right uphill, through a pretty patchwork of gardens where, at the right season, oranges and lemons ripen in the shelter of rubble walls and cane windbreaks. After climbing for about ten minutes, come to a TRACK at the base of the cliff on the west side of the valley (**2h40min**). Follow this for five minutes, then turn right on asphalt and, in a few minutes, turn right again onto the OLD RAMLA ('BAY') ROAD. After bearing left in five minutes and left again three minutes later, the road peters out into a path at a group of farmhouses on the edge of the cliff overlooking Ir-Ramla (**2h55min**). Just past the FARMHOUSE WITH A SHRINE AND LAMP, take a path that leads down to a track that exits 40m/yds from the beach on the MAIN ROAD. As you descend, savour the extensive views of the valley leading to the bay and the coast. The sweep of red-gold sand lapped by an impossibly

*In wet weather, the climb out of San Blas Bay is very slippery; take this alternative route. Instead of turning right at Villa San Blas, go straight ahead for a minute, to a viewpoint with seats. Descend to the valley on a very narrow road and reach a crossroads where Triq Wied Bingemma comes down the

valley on your left. Continue straight ahead, climbing steadily. At about the 9min-mark, turn right to the old Ramla Bay road (12min). Pick up the main walk just before the 2h30min-point. This reduces overall walking time by approximately 20min.

Prickly pear cacti leaves are used as little individual wind-breaks to protect young seedlings in the San Blas Valley.

blue sea makes a picnic at **Ir-Ramla** (**3h05min**; Picnic 26e, photograph page 33) irresistible. Roman remains (villa and viaduct) also add interest, as does the so-called Calypso's Cave on the hill.

From the bay, turn up the main valley road. Ignore the first road to the right but, in a further 200m/yds, take the *next* right turn (where the main road swings left; **3h10min**). Continue past a series of DAMS and turn left on a track (where the road begins to climb towards Xaghra; **3h35min**). Fifteen minutes later, turn right uphill on a track. A small stone building is off to the left just past this junction. Pass a POND on the left, some 100m/yds up the track, an

electricity pole on the right. The track winds through small fields, springs and more ponds and exits on a road on the outskirts of **Xaghra** (TRIQ IT-TAFLA; **3h57min**). The route to the neolithic temples of Ggantija involves turning right towards the centre of Xaghra. Continue straight on in one minute (at the next junction) into TRIQ PARISOT, left in a further three minutes into TRIQ JOHN OTTO BAYER and left again two minutes later (TRIQ L-IMQADES). The entrance to **Ggantija** is less than two minutes along this street (**4h05min**). You can catch a bus nearby on the main XAGHRA/XEWKIJA ROAD to Mgarr via Marsalforn and change at Marsalforn for the bus to Victoria.

**An optional detour offers the opportunity to explore local agriculture and traditional irrigation techniques in the small rock gardens close to the Mistra Rocks which lie between San Blas Bay and Dahlet Qorrot. Just before the bottom of the road, where the main walk forks left, bear right. Follow the road to its end at a turning point (5min). Follow the higher track (ignoring any paths to lower plots on your left) to an irrigation tank overlooked by a large boulder. Ahead lie the fear-

some Mistra Rocks, huge boulders interspersed with thorny bushes. Return to the turning point. The left-hand path, on slightly lower ground, leads to another irrigation tank at the edge of the cultivated area. *From here a faintly defined path leads into the rocks, but don't be tempted to explore one of the least-visited parts of the islands — there are crevasses, dangerous crumbling, man-made walls and the risk of losing your way. Allow an extra* 20min *for the higher route and* 35min *for both routes.*

Walk 27 COMINO: WALKS FROM THE COMINO HOTEL, SAN NIKLAW BAY

See also photographs pages 7, 9
Distance: 9.1km/5.7mi;
2h30min
Grade: easy, with an overall
ascent/descent of 205m/675ft
Equipment: stout shoes, sunhat,
swimwear, waterproofs, water
How to get there and return:
There are two choices; see page
133:

⚓ A ferry service between
Cirkewwa or Mgarr (Gozo) and
Comino is operated by the
Comino Hotel from mid-March
to mid-November. Please note
that the Comino Hotel offers a
day package to non-residents.
This includes the ferry trip,
lunch and use of the hotel
facilities. Places are limited, and
you should telephone 24h in
advance to make a reservation.
The main walk begins and ends
at the hotel slipway. Should you
decide not to purchase the hotel
package, you can still travel on
their boat if space is available.

⚓ United Comino Ferries run a
scheduled service to the Blue
Lagoon from Marfa (near the
Riviera Hotel) and Cirkewwa
(adjacent kiosk on the North
Quay). There are fewer sailings

in winter — and the service may
be cancelled in poor weather.
Do check sailing times and
weather conditions before
travelling to Marfa or Cirkewwa
(see pages 132-133 for details).
Alternative walk 1
(7.5km/4.7mi; 2h; easy, with an
overall ascent/descent of
175m/575ft). *This route is
designed for visitors to Comino
who have not purchased the
hotel package but have travelled
on the hotel boat.* Follow the
main walk to the Blue Lagoon,
Comino Tower and the Isolation
Hospital. Carry straight on at the
six cottages, using the notes on
page 130 to end the walk.
Alternative walk 2 (4.8km/3mi;
1h20min; easy, with an overall
ascent/descent of 105m/350ft).
*This walk is intended for those
who have taken a trip to the
Blue Lagoon.* Follow the main
walk from the 8min-point to
Comino Tower and the old
Isolation Hospital, then carry
straight on to Santa Marija Bay,
ignoring the left turn at the
cottages. Make your way back
to the Blue Lagoon by the same
route.

Comino is the third island in the archipelago and has
a unique atmosphere ... few residents and hardly any
vehicles! It is the ideal place to go on a fine Sunday, when
Malta's roads are choked with traffic, and huge queues at
the ferry terminals frustrate travel to and from Gozo. The
island derives its name from cumin, a herb similar to
fennel. Peace and quiet prevail here, helped by the
island's status as a bird sanctuary.

Since it is most convenient to
arrive aboard the Comino
Hotel's boat, the walk starts at
their SLIPWAY, returns to this
point for lunch (see notes under
'How to get there'), and ends up
here for the trip home.
Start out by following the track

uphill out of the Hotel's private
grounds. When you come to a
building with a BLUE DOOR
(**3min**), turn right. In about five
minutes you reach the western
coast and the famous **Blue
Lagoon** (**8min**; Picnic 27;
photograph page 9), with its

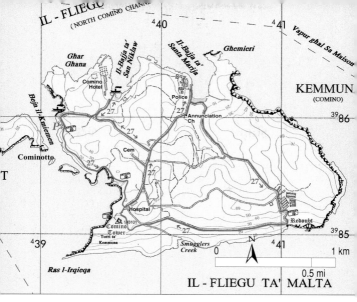

IL - FLIEGU TA' MALTA

iridescent green- and blue-hued waters. In high season a fleet of yachts and cruise boats from Malta will be anchored here, but happily part of the lagoon is roped off for the exclusive use of swimmers. This is becoming a very popular spot, and there is a toilet/shower block and mobile vans supply refreshments to visitors.

Continue along the coastal footpath, keeping well away from the overhanging cliff-edges, and enjoy the spectacle of indigo sea, brooding caves and the offshore islets (Cominotto being the first and largest of them). Continue on around two small bays, avoiding the enclosed depression between them which exits directly to the sea. At **30min** the path turns up right to **Comino Tower** (built in 1618). For a wonderful view over the island and out to Malta and Gozo, climb the tower, crossing the rickety drawbridge. Although not open to the public, you can walk round the exterior at entrance door level. *Take care:*

there is no fencing, and it is unsuitable for children.
The old **Isolation Hospital** is your next port of call. In the corner of one wing some dusty crates of empty bottles are a reminder of the time when an old lady kept a bar here!

The track now runs north, and the curious may wish to divert to the old cemetery on the hill; otherwise continue straight ahead, until you reach DESERTED COTTAGES grouped around a compound. About 50m/yds before the cottages, turn left and follow a wide track which gradually descends past a patchwork of walled and cane-edged fields to **San Niklaw Bay**. This is a pretty, but private beach, belonging to the Comino Hotel. You've now walked for almost **1h** and should be ready for a buffet lunch and a swim (included in your day-trip package).

Suitably refreshed, retrace your steps to the track junction near the COTTAGES and turn left. Fifteen minutes from the hotel you come to a tiny CHURCH

129

Comino Tower

of the PIG FARM, which was built to restock Maltese farms after the 1980 swine-fever epidemic. Turn right here and, almost immediately, turn left on a narrower track, keeping the buildings of the pig farm on your left. Past here the track drops steeply towards the South Comino Channel. Turn left to visit the restored **Santa Marija Battery** which was built in 1715. You can explore the interior and the ramparts, provided the access gate is open (**1h40min** — or 40min after lunch).

(where services are still held), surrounded by trees (**1h15min**). The POLICE STATION, which is concealed above a little boat-house and slipway, is your next target, reached two minutes later. Carry on to the 'South Sea Island' Beach, **Santa Marija**, fringed with tamarisk trees and vitex shrubs. Walk along the beach, then cut inland on a track leading uphill just beyond the public CAMPING SITE (some 80m/yds before a jetty). You pass **Comino Major**, rising to all of 75m/247ft on the left. The next landmark on this section of the walk are the extensive but disused buildings

Leaving the battery, continue along the coast on a good track which runs about 30m/100ft above the gently-sloping south coast of the island. In **2h** (1h after lunch) come to a turning down to **Smugglers Creek**, in which according to local legend lies the wreck of a small ship laden with contraband cigarettes.

Soon you're back at **Comino Tower**. Retrace your steps to the HOTEL; some **2h30min** (or 1h30min after lunch) should find you there.

The old Isolation Hospital

BUS AND FERRY INFORMATION

MALTA

Arriva Bus Malta Ltd (Triq L-Imdina, Qormi) operate a scheduled bus service from Valletta, Sliema, Bugibba and Rabat throughout Malta and from Victoria in Gozo. The latest timetable information is given on their website www.arriva. com.mt (tel: 2122 2000; e-mail: enquiries@arriva.co.mt). Below I list selected services for getting to and from the walks and picnics in this book, as well as handy routes serving the resorts.

Bus Services from VALLETTA

Destination	Route	Average frequency	Last bus from destination
Bahar ic-Caghaq[1]	11/12	10min	23.15
Birzebbuga	82	20min	22.13
Bugibba[2]	31	10min	23.00
Cirkewwa (for	11/41	30min	22.35
Gozo and Comino ferries)/Mellieha[3]	X6	hourly	22.50
Cospicua/Vittoriosa	2	10min	23.08
Dingli	52	30min	22.50
Ghajn Tuffieha/ Golden Bay/Mgarr	23	30min	22.36
Gharghur	21/23	20min	22.36
Marsascala	91	10min	22.55
Marsaxlokk	81	20min	22.57
Mosta	21/23/31/41	10-20min	23.05
Naxxar	43	15min	22.46
Qrendi	72	30min	22.30
Rabat/Mdina	51/52/53	10-20min	23.00
St Julian's/Paceville	11/12/13	5-10min	23.30
Senglea	1	20-30min	22.36
Siggiewi	62	30min	22.45
Sliema Ferries	11/12/13	5-10min	23.40
Xghajra	3	hourly	23.12
Zurrieq	71	15min	22.45

Selected express and direct bus services in Malta

X1: Airport/Marsa Park & Ride/Pembroke Park & Ride-Mellieha (Belle View) interchange/Cirkewwa, 05.35-22.45, at least hourly
Last bus departs Cirkewwa 22.45; Mellieha (Belle View) 22.59

Feeder service **102:** Gnejna/Mgarr/Bingemma/Ghajn Tuffieha/Golden Bay/ Manikata/Mellieha (Belle View) interchange and in reverse direction, hourly except Bingemma served from Mgarr once every two hours; to Mgarr once every two hours
Last bus with onward connection at Mgarr departs Ghajn Tuffieha 21.48

Feeder service **107:** Rabat/Buskett/Dingli/Ta' Qali/Stadium/Rabat, hourly
Last bus departs Dingli 22.27; Buskett 22.34

[1] Served by services to Bugibba
[2] Also served by services to Cirkewwa
[3] Last 🚌 X6 departs Mellieha (Belle View) interchange 23.10; also served by 🚌 X1 Cirkewwa/Pembroke/Airport with last departure at 22.59

Route **109:** Rabat/Siggiewi/Ghar Lapsi, hourly
Last bus departs Ghar Lapsi 22.30

Route **124:** Vittoriosa/Cospicua/Zabbar/Marsacala/St Thomas, hourly
Last bus departs St Thomas 22.54

Route **135:** Gudja/Airport/Luqa/Marsa Park & Ride/University (Tal-Qroqq), hourly
Last bus departs Gudja 22.20 with onward connection at University on route 31 to Valletta or Bugibba

Route **201:** Bahrija/Rabat/Siggiewi/Zurrieq/Airport, hourly
Last bus departs Bahrija 21.49; Blue Grotto 22.52

Route 202: St Julian's interchange/Sliema Ferries/Mosta-Ta' Qali/Rabat/Mdina, every 30min
Last bus departs Rabat/Mdina 22.25

GOZO

The walks in this book have been written up for easy access from Malta. Two of the walks begin at Mgarr harbour; the other two start from Victoria, after a short journey on either the No 301 or 303 bus from Mgarr.

Bus services from Victoria and Mgarr harbour

Route **301:** Victoria/Xewkija/Mgarr 05.25-22.55, every 30min;
Mgarr/Xewkija/Victoria 05.55-22.55, every 30min

Route **302:** Dwejra/San Lawrenz/Victoria/Xewkija/Ramla 05.21-22.21, hourly from Victoria to Dwejra; 06.00-22.00, hourly from Victoria to Ramla
Last bus departs Dwejra 22.39; Ramla 22.35

Route **303:** Victoria/Nadur/Qala/Mgarr 05.40-22.40, hourly;
Mgarr/Qala/Nadur/ Victoria 06.10-22.10, hourly

Route **305:** Victoria/San Lawrenz/Gharb/Victoria 05.55-22.55, hourly from Victoria
Departs Gharb 06.11 -23.11

Route **306:** Xlendi/Victoria/Marsalforn/Qbbajjar 05.35-22.35, hourly from Victoria to Xlendi; 05.58-22.58, hourly from Victoria to Marsalforn/Qabbajjar
Last bus departs Xlendi 22.45; Qbajjar 23.12

Route **309:** Victoria/Zebbug/Stivali/Victoria 05.30-22.30, hourly from Victoria
Last bus departs Zebbug 22.42

Route **322:** Mgarr/Nadur/Xaghra/Marsalforn/Mgarr 05.40-22.40, hourly from Mgarr to Marsalforn
Departs Xaghra 6.00-22.00; Marsalforn 6.10-22.10

Malta-Gozo ferry service

This service is operated by roll-on/roll-off vehicle ferries belonging to the Gozo Channel Company, Channel House, Mgarr Harbour, Mgarr, Gozo (www.gozochannel.com; tel: 2210 9000; e-mail: admin@gozochannel.com). The trip from Cirkewwa at the northern tip of Malta to Mgarr harbour takes about 25 minutes. Sailings operate at 45 minute intervals between 05.45 (Malta departures) and 06.00 (Gozo departures) until 21.45 and at a frequency of approximately 1h30min at other times.

Comino boat services (passenger only)

Comino Hotel boat: The service is operated by the Comino Hotels between mid-March and mid-November (www.cominohotel.com; tel: 2152 9821; e-mail info@cominohotel.com).
Note that arriving and departing hotel guests are given preference on this boat.

Malta/Comino/Malta
Departs Cirkewwa: 07.30, 10.00, 16.45, 18.30
Departs Comino: 06.40 (via Gozo), 09.40, 16.15, 18.05

Gozo/Comino/Gozo
Departs Mgarr: 06.15, 08.30, 11.05, 15.00, 15.45, 17.50, 22.00
Departs Comino: 08.10, 10.30, 14.30, 17.30, 21.15 *(on request)*, 24.00

United Comino Ferries: White Haven, Triq Cordina, Ghajnsielem, Gozo (www.cominoferries.com; tel: 9940 6529; 9947 4142; e-mail info@cominoferries.com).

Departs Marfa (opposite Riviera Hotel) 9.00, 10.00, 11.00, 12.00, 13.00, 14.00, 15.00, 16.30

Departs Cirkewwa (adjacent kiosk, North Quay) 9.10, 10.10, 11.00, 12.10, 13.10, 14.10, 15.10, 16.40

Departs Blue Lagoon, Comino 9.30, 10.30, 11.30, 12.30, 13.30, 14.30, 15.30, 16.30, 17.30

Please note that a limited service is operated in the winter months.

● Index

Geographical names comprise the only entries in this index. For other entries, see
Contents, page 3. Maltese place names (see page 31) follow the better-known English
names which have been used in the text. Some place names *not* used in the text are
also included. A page number in *italic type* indicates a map reference; a page number
in **bold type** indicates a photograph. Either of these may be in addition to a text
reference on the same page. (M) = Malta, (G) = Gozo, (C) = Comino. See also Bus
and Ferry timetables, beginning on page 131.